Last Chance Garage

With the assistance of
William G. Scheller

Illustrations by
ANCO/Boston

Photography by
Michael Lutch

1817

Harper & Row, Publishers, New York   Cambridge, Philadelphia, San Francisco,
London, Mexico City, São Paulo, Sydney
1984

LAST Garage CHANCE

A system-by-system guide to understanding how your car runs, why it occasionally doesn't, and what to do about it.

by Brad Sears

First Edition

*Library of Congress Cataloging in
Publication Data*

Sears, Brad.
        Last chance garage.

        Includes index.
        1. Automobiles — Maintenance
        and repair — Amateurs' man-
        uals.   2. Automobiles.

I. Title.
TL152.S434   1984   629.2.28′722   83-48803
ISBN 0-06-015309-1
ISBN 0-06-091139-5 (pbk.)

*To a mechanic's mechanic, Ralph Sears
(1903-1983)*

Preface

Welcome to *Last Chance Garage!* Some of you will already be familiar with our television program, produced by WGBH-TV in Boston and seen throughout the United States on the stations of the Public Broadcasting System. We'd like to think of this book as a companion to the show — not so much a compilation in print and pictures of what we've done on the air, but a guide to automotive systems, maintenance, and repair that will serve as both background and elaboration on our weekly televised demonstrations. Of course, you don't need a television to get the most out of the book. You just need an automobile and a little curiosity about what makes it run. I've had that curiosity all my life, and it has helped me get an immeasurable amount of fun out of driving. It's never been completely satisfied, though hardly a week goes by when I don't learn something new about cars.

If there's one thing I'd like to convey aside from specific information about transmissions, ignition systems, disc brakes, and the like, it is a positive attitude about automobile ownership. Too many of us assume an adversary relationship with our cars. To a certain degree this attitude has been fostered by critics who simply don't like automobiles to begin with, but even more so it comes from feeling betrayed when something goes wrong with a part or system that may have worked flawlessly for many thousands of miles. When you think about how complicated an automobile is, and how many things it can do for us, it's easier to forgive the occasional mechanical lapse. And if you know how to fix it — or where to get it competently fixed — even more of the sting is taken away.

Those are the ideas behind *Last Chance Garage*, and it has taken the efforts of more than one person to bring them to life in the television series and in

this book. I'd especially like to thank Bill Scheller, who oversaw translation of the materials from garage and studio formats to the printed page, and without whose assistance this book would never have been written. Grateful thanks are due the people at Fram Corporation, whose enthusiasm and generous funding made the television series possible — in particular, Frank McGonigle, Vice President, Advertising; Karen Borger, Public Relations Manager; and Dave Bowman, Technical Communications Manager, and technical advisor/editor to the program and book. I am indebted to Christopher Gilbert, executive producer, and Eleanor Jewett, producer/director, of the production team at WGBH Boston, whose skills and tireless efforts have contributed so much to the success of the television series. Materials, parts, labor and memorabilia for photos in this book were generously loaned to us by Robert C. English; C. Ashton Cox; Tire Shack of East Taunton, Massachusetts; the West Warwick, Rhode Island branch of American Discount Auto Parts (ADAP); Fitzmaurice Lincoln Mercury, Brockton, Massachusetts; Heritage Plantation of Sandwich, Massachusetts; Tony Naden's Lockshop at Dickson Brothers Hardware, Cambridge, Massachusetts; and the Sign Shop of the Metropolitan District Commission, Commonwealth of Massachusetts. Finally, grateful appreciation to my son and daughter-in-law, Steve and Sherry Sears, who have contributed enormously to our media and consulting ventures.

Contents

Introduction

For twenty-five years before there was a "Last Chance Garage," I worked at the business of selling, maintaining, and repairing automobiles. During that time I dealt with new cars, used cars, everything from engines to bodywork — and met just about every type of person and every kind of problem a mechanic can encounter. Some of my biggest headaches in those days came from trying to undo jobs that had been poorly done by other mechanics, and from trying to coax accurate descriptions of symptoms from customers who really hadn't been educated to listen to and carefully relate an automobile's warning signals of trouble. I came out of those years of experience with what I believed to be a pretty good understanding of the way things ought to be done and with a desire to put that knowledge to work.

I began my teaching efforts in high school vocational-education programs. I was frustrated, though, by the fact that a good many high school kids come into auto-maintenance courses because of a combination of career indecision and a fascination with fast cars. Unfortunately, that isn't enough. I found myself spending too much time babysitting and puttering along with menial projects. I decided that this wasn't quite the route I wanted to take and got involved instead with running service clinics for professional mechanics. I still find this very rewarding, although the audience is necessarily limited. It was the media — print and later electronic — that finally gave me the satisfaction of educating as many people as possible to what I feel is important about car ownership and maintenance.

My first media effort was a popular column called "Shop Talk," which ran for over ten years in the buff-oriented newspaper *Old Cars*. It covered common problems and taught people how to do their own repair work. I then began writing the road-test and question-and-answer columns that still appear in a host of U.S. newspapers.

Radio came next. Between 1973 and 1977, Boston stations WMEX and WITS carried my "Automobile Doctor" talk shows, and in 1977 I joined WEEI, a CBS-owned Boston station, to do a series of spots called "At Your Service for Car Owners," which remain on the air today.

In 1979, Russ Morash of Public Broadcasting's WGBH-TV, Channel 2 in Boston, began talking to me about the possibility of doing a local television show about cars. The idea was to teach people about their automobiles and about automobile servicing. We would want our viewers to learn how to evaluate mechanics and their work, how to recognize good and bad cars, both new and used, and in general to take an informed approach to the hard decisions associated with this universal — yet universally misunderstood — form of transportation. Out of those initial discussions grew the nationwide "Last Chance Garage" show, with Russ applying the same creative powers and television savvy that have led to his development of such outstanding WGBH productions as "The French Chef" and subsequent Julia Child shows, "The Victory Garden," and "This Old House." Having concept, title and "look" of the show in such extraordinary hands created the opportunity for me to have a lot of fun while offering a lifetime of automobile experience to the television audience.

•

These are troubled times for the automobile industry in the United States. The manufacturers' problems have been pretty well documented, but the situation extends to service operations as well.

Sources within the federal government have recently alleged that as much as 50 percent of the consumer's automobile dollar is wasted. This contention has been taken up by followers of activists such as Ralph Nader and Joan Claybrook, who argue that if this expenditure is wasted, it follows that consumers are the victims of a mass ripoff and that the whole industry — from manufacturers to garage owners — is totally dishonest. I disagree with this attitude. I believe that to be fair, we should break that 50-percent "waste" estimate down into three categories.

The first category contains the money lost to undeniable ripoff artists, mechanics who are consciously out to pick your pockets. There is no excuse for these characters, and no defense against them except sound consumer education.

The ripoff in the second category isn't quite so deliberate. There are practicing mechanics who simply don't know how to diagnose and repair an automobile, and whose misdiagnoses and faulty or unnecessary repairs can cost you a lot of money. It's the job of TV programs such as "Last Chance Garage," and of my newspaper columns and radio shows, to inform consumers as to how to spot and stay away from not only the pickpockets, but also the operators whose unconscious fleecing of the public stems from their own professional incompetence.

Finally, we have the problem of communication, which may well be responsible for the biggest share of wasted car-repair dollars. Time and time again, in attempting to resolve complaints between a consumer and a garage owner, I find that there has been a lack of meaningful communication between the two. Here's an example. A car owner is aware of certain symptoms — a peculiar noise, or a skip in the engine — that spell trouble. He brings his car into the shop and says to the mechanic, "Tune it up. I'll be back at five." He comes back at five, finds that the car has been tuned, and takes it out on the road to find that the symptoms are still present. Who's at fault here? The car owner told the mechanic what he wanted done, and the mechanic did it. But he didn't say *why* he wanted it done, nor did he make any attempt to describe the problem that brought him in, in the first place. Because he didn't tell the mechanic what he wanted corrected, it didn't get corrected.

The preceding is not an example of a ripoff. At worst, it's an unconscious ripoff that stems from a simple absence of communication. The responsibility has to be shared between the consumer and the mechanic (after all, the former didn't tell the whole story, but the latter didn't ask for it either).

The goal of *Last Chance Garage*, both on the air and in this book, is to tell people how and why an automobile works the way it does and to suggest how to talk to and deal with professional mechanics. The members of that much-maligned breed are all human like the rest of us, and most of them are not out to rob you deliberately. Learn how to communicate with them, and you'll probably get good work done at reasonable prices. If we can bring the consumer and the industry a little closer together and help people to maintain their cars with a little less pain and fewer wasted dollars, then this "garage" will have done its job.

You and Your Mechanic: Life Doesn't Have to Be Difficult

For all its joys and conveniences, owning a car has its exasperating moments as well. And most of us will agree that the most trying times of all are not associated with parking spaces, tickets, or shelling out at the gas pump, but with repairs. Cars are inconsiderate. They can break down at the worst possible times, forcing an instant decision or series of decisions about what to do next. This chapter is about those decisions and how you can educate yourself to make them when your next trip has to be a trip to the garage.

In the best of all possible worlds, you could take your ailing automobile down to the Last Chance Garage and we'd fix you right up. In the world we do live in, things aren't quite so simple. If the breakdown occurs in your home court, you'll probably have a local mechanic whom you have used in the past, or at least be able to go to a nearby garage recommended by friends and neighbors. But many of us move around a lot and may not have had car trouble since changing addresses. Or, trouble may come along when you're out on the road. How do you go about finding a garage and making the acquaintance of a good mechanic? Here are some guidelines, beginning with a few basic definitions of just what type of automobile-repair establishments are out there.

Chains, Dealers, and Independents

Nearly all garages fall into one of three categories: chains, dealerships, and independents. Each has its specialties and peculiarities, each its pros and cons.

When we speak of *chains*, we're talking about the service centers operated by tire manufacturers such as Goodyear and Firestone, discount and department-store operations such as the ones associated with K-Mart or Sears, Roebuck outlets, and the big national specialty franchises such as Midas and Aamco. Let's take a look at each of these groups.

One of the big differences between the "tire store" operations and the discount chain garages has to do with the parts they package and sell. The tire stores sell a brand name — their own — attached to parts that they purchase through a "private labeling" arrangement with a high-quality manufacturer. For instance, the air filter you buy at the Goodyear service center will say "Goodyear" on it (or at least on the box), yet it will have been made by one of the big filter companies who sell elsewhere under their own name.

The discount chains stock their parts a little differently. What you find on the shelves in their garages is usually predicated on price — that is, the chain will shop around among both domestic and foreign parts manufacturers for the best deal on merchandise that they can then package and sell under their house label. As a result, you're not always sure of getting the same product under the same label every time you buy, and the quality may well vary. Now, don't neglect to make the distinction here between house labels and the well-recognized national brands, some of which are also offered by the discount chains. If the box says "Fram," then the oil filter in it was made by Fram. If it has the discounter's house label on it, it may have been made by one company one month, another the next. This may not always matter a great deal, but sometimes, when parts of the highest quality are important to the functioning of the car, the difference can be crucial. Several of the late-model imports, for instance, have extremely stringent oil-filter requirements — if they aren't met, oil-pump pressure can blow the filter off and the engine may be ruined. So, if your car is at all fussy about its parts, the discount house may not be the best place to buy them. If the discounter does sell name-brand items, though, he may well sell them more cheaply. It all depends on his buying power and on the extent to which he wants to use the name-brand part as a "loss leader" to get you into his store.

Chains and discount operations also differ from dealerships and independent garages when it comes to specialization — the practice of limiting the type of service offered to one or two of the more basic repair categories. We're all familiar with the big nationwide companies that specialize in, say, mufflers or rebuilt transmissions. But apart from these there are the discount and tire-store garages whose services seldom go beyond tire, brake, and front-end work, garden-variety tuneups, and other such "gravy jobs." Sticking to these areas gives these companies a better opportunity to hold up the bottom line. It also gives the service managers the chance to "build" an individual job — for instance, a front-end repair — with profitable parts such as tie rods, idler arms, and ball joints. When a discount shop can stick to one line of repairs involving one line of parts on which there is a comfortable markup, it is likely to stay a lot more profitable on the balance sheets of the company that runs it.

Dealerships and independents, on the other hand, offer a more complete line of service. You can drive in for a brake job or a muffler or a tuneup one week, and be just as welcome the following week when you show up with a more difficult and labor-intensive engine or electrical problem. (Some independents, of course, build up a reputation in one specialized area, such as carburetors or transmissions, and are the sorts of places you'd probably go to on the recommendation of another local independent who does not make a regular business of that particular specialty.) You may pay a little bit more for those gravy jobs that the discount store out on the highway could have handled, but aside from being able to count on a more predictable line of name-brand parts, you also get a chance to build up a relationship with a garage that will be able to handle just about any type of job you come in with.

So, where do you go? Undeniably, there are things that some chains do well. Some of the franchised muffler installers, for example, are capable of high-quality work at an attractive price and with a sound guarantee. But there are some clear disadvantages to dealing consistently with tire stores and discount chains. One of these is the level of training and experience you can expect from the people who staff the chain garage. The discounters set service-department salary levels that are usually unattractively low for a trained mechanic. This means that the shop becomes a training ground for inexperienced mechanics — but the problem is, there's usually no one in the shop who can provide the proper training. If a chain does attempt to provide its own training program, it will most often draw upon its own merchandising personnel, with a smattering of assistance from the manufacturers of the parts it sells. The quality of this type of training will vary. But the larger problem may well have to do with the trainees themselves. Most of the would-be master mechanics who are worth their salt aren't going to want to make themselves available for the barely-above-minimum wages the chains usually pay, and are going to sign on with a dealership or an independent instead.

The big liability in dealing with discount chain garages, though, has to do not with the quality of their parts and workmanship but with what happens when you have a problem that they aren't equipped to deal with. For instance, you've gotten into the habit of going to the discounter for tires, lubes, alignments, and tuneups, but suddenly you're faced with a ring job or a worn clutch. Now you've got to find someone who does engine work or clutch replacement, and that person is going to be the dealer or the independent. However, he hasn't been seeing you for the routine work — the gravy jobs that you've been farming out to the discount garage. The dealer or the independent is going to know right away that you're not a regular customer; he's going to see the discounter's name on your tires or on your antifreeze tag, and spot the house-brand filters and spark plugs that you've been using. He's going to think, "Here's somebody that didn't want to know me when he needed a tuneup or a front-end job, but now that he's got a problem the discounter can't fix, look who he comes to." You're starting off without the rapport that means so much in dealings between a mechanic and a customer. Was it worth it, for the little you may have been saving on the smaller jobs?

What about dealerships? You often hear it said that as soon as your warranty expires, and you're no longer required to have your work done by the dealer, you should start taking your car somewhere else. This is by no means a necessary rule to live by. The time was when you could pretty much expect that the dealer's service department would charge the highest rates in town, perhaps one-third more than the independents. But that has been changing, and it's much more common now for all of the shops in a given area to come within a dollar or two of each other on their hourly rates. What's more, the dealer is almost always likely to quote you a price based on flat rate. Flat rate, as we'll learn in a more detailed discussion of pricing practices later in this chapter, is a system of uniform job pricing geared to the standard length of time estimated for the performance of each repair job.

Another thing the dealer has going for him is his familiarity with your particular make of car. Things have been changing so rapidly, in Detroit and in the foreign automotive capitals, that the company-sponsored training seminars and frequent service bulletins that the dealers receive constitute the best means of keeping up with the latest design changes and engineering developments. However, the more dedicated and competitive independents also make a point of keeping their eyes and ears open. Often, an independent garage owner will build up a reputation for expertise with a certain model or a certain range of model years. This may be just what you need if you have an aging automobile and no recent dealer affiliation.

In addition to training, the dealerships will often excel in the type and variety of equipment they have at their disposal. Except in the odd case (there's always an exception to the rule), the manufacturer that a dealer represents is not going to let him get away with running a "screwdriver and flashlight" shop that lacks the machinery necessary to perform important repair tasks.

You're also likely to find sophisticated equipment in a discount shop, since its purchase represents a capital outlay that works in the corporate owner's favor at tax time. But there's often an important difference between the machinery at the dealer's garage and the same equipment down at the discounter's. The difference is not in the nuts and bolts and levers and dials, but in the expertise of the service technicians who operate all this expensive gadgetry. One of the discount chains, for example, has what is probably the most sophisticated battery/alternator/starter testing equipment in the world. The trouble is, maybe no more than five of the people who work for this outfit nationwide know how to use it. The wages these companies offer, and the resulting high rate of employee turnover, pretty much guarantee that few of the people in this kind of shop are going to care enough, or be around long enough, to get the full potential from the equipment on hand.

Depending on his resources and how conscientious he is, the independent may also have an investment in the kind of sophisticated equipment that helps make the difference between standard and superior service. Of course, he is on his own to a greater extent than the dealership mechanic when it comes to getting training — a subject we'll take a closer look at later. For now, remember that one of the basic requirements of a good garage is

that it have enough equipment to service your car properly. For instance, if an independent mechanic offers tuneup service, he should have tuneup machines and not just a light and a couple of hand tools. Ideally, he would have an electronic engine analyzer, including an oscilloscope and the accompanying gauges. This and any other specialized machinery should occupy a prominent position in the shop and should look like it's being used — there's no good reason for it to be stuck back in a corner and covered with dirt and old rags, or wheeled out only in the case of severe diagnostic problems.

Tuneup equipment like this can make the difference between standard and superior service — if the service technician who operates the sophisticated electronic gadgets is an expert.

What to Look for in a Garage

We've covered the different types of garages: chains, dealers, and independents. But that still leaves a vast range of choices among individual shops in each category. In making your way through the thick of them, general word-of-mouth and the advice of trusted acquaintances will be invaluable. But there are a number of objective criteria you should know about and that you can use as yardsticks in sizing up one garage against another.

Once again, we're back to the subject of training. Is the mechanic you're considering certified by the National Institute for Automotive Service Excellence (NIASE)? Are there any diplomas hang-

National Institute for AUTOMOTIVE SERVICE EXCELLENCE ®

ing on his walls, verifying his attendance at clinics covering such areas as engine tuneup, charging systems, carburetor overhauls, or air conditioning? If a mechanic has attended clinics or schools, he'll usually post his diplomas — and if you don't see any, don't be afraid to ask. Usually, you'll get one of two answers. He'll say yes, and tell you which ones he's been to, or he'll say something like, "No, those things are useless, I don't believe in them," in which case, you might do well to look up another mechanic. If he does keep up on his training, he'll usually be happy

that you asked about it, because it's a sign that someone is taking an interest in his world. So, don't be shy.

What's wrong with the mechanic who doesn't occasionally go back for some brushup training or take steps to learn about the latest developments in the cars he services? It's a good bet that he's liable to be a replacement artist — he'll do a passable job of taking out one part and putting in another. But when it comes to a tough diagnostic problem, especially on a new car, he's the man who will scratch his head, throw up his hands, and begin a series of trial-by-error replacements that will cost you money. Obviously, it's better that he should learn what's going on in a clinic instead of while working on your car, with his clock ticking off an hourly rate that you have to pay. But with his know-it-all, can't-teach-me-anything attitude, it isn't likely to happen.

That penchant for replacement rather than repair, incidentally, is one of the things that plagues the patrons of chain operations specializing in specific components — most notoriously, transmissions. When you go to a chain, be prepared to have ailing parts completely replaced, even if they might have been entirely salvageable. The people who staff these shops are trained to take out a transmission, disassemble and clean it, replace whatever appears to be malfunctioning, put it all back together, and reinstall it in the car. If this doesn't work, they'll remove the transmission again, take out all the new parts they put in, discard the rest of the old transmission, and install an off-the-shelf rebuilt unit. You'll have two choices: the regular rebuild, at one price, and the "lifetime" rebuild, which may easily cost a couple of hundred dollars more. In most cases, the transmissions are the same — it's the guarantee that you pay for. Nor is the "free evaluation" much of a bargain. Once the chain man has the pan off and has told you what work he thinks you need, you'll usually be charged for putting it all back together if you decide you don't want the work done. What all this points to is that your best bet for transmission repair is either the dealer or the independent who does nothing but transmissions. If your regular mechanic doesn't handle the work, he will recommend someone who does. The mechanic you get sent to will almost surely be as competent as the one who gave the reference, because no garage keeper wants a steady customer coming back hollering about the shoddy work done by someone he has recommended.

Now, let's say you've listened to the advice of your neighbors, done some scouting around on your own, and settled on a garage that you feel you can trust. The next question might be, Can you go into that garage and ask for the services of a specific mechanic? This might have been a moot point at one time, when one-man shops were far more prevalent than they are nowadays. With today's overhead, a mechanic working alone has a very hard time turning a profit. You're far more likely to encounter a shop with three to six workers, although some independent operations in big metropolitan areas can employ as many as fifty.

Out of a crew of three, four, or maybe a half-dozen workers in a shop, you may be familiar with one individual who has done good work on your car in the past and whom you'd like to have take care of other problems as they arise. When you think about it, this is the same thing you do in a barber shop or beauty salon. There's no reason not to follow the same procedure in dealing with a garage — but by all means, make your arrangements through the owner or manager of the shop, and don't try to "pirate" a particular mechanic by going to him behind the manager's back and asking if he'll work on your car over the weekend. The pirate theory is simple, and it's even been recommended in a couple of recent books on car ownership and repair. It goes like this: if you pay the mechanic a price somewhere between what the shop pays him and what the shop charges you, you'll both come out ahead. Sounds fine — but in practice, it just isn't fair. The owner of the garage has a right to make a living, and for someone who pays for rent, heat, electricity, insurance, and tools, that means turning a profit. He can't continue to run a good shop and offer you high-quality service if you steal his help. If it's a matter of common knowledge that the helper

The Village Smithy

The auto industry is less than one century old, but it is one of the most important to the country. The repair segment of the industry grows out of a once-familiar institution in every city and hamlet from coast to coast: the village blacksmith.

The smithy was a logical choice to take care of the new-fangled contraptions. He was the man who knew the most about machinery, as he and he alone kept the grain mills and other machinery in each village running.

The terms we hear today in the auto industry reflect this heritage — for example, "I guess it's time for a new car. Might as well get down to some serious horse trading." After all, who also took care of the livery stable and the horses? The village smithy, that's who.

mechanic runs an aboveboard business of his own on the side, that's a different story, particularly if he specializes in something that the big shop doesn't handle, or doesn't handle as well.

Now, suppose you're playing by the rules, and you approach the shop manager and ask that a specific mechanic do the work on your car. He'll say either yes or no. If he turns you down for no good reason, you might wish to reconsider your patronage of that garage. But there might be any number of perfectly legitimate reasons why you can't pick and choose your mechanic on a given day. The simplest one is that the fellow might be busy — shop managers book jobs into their garages for certain hours of the day and days of the week and assign their helpers accordingly. In a situation like that, when the manager says, "No, Fred's busy," ask him when Fred will be free and make your appointment for that time. (This tactic does not apply, of course, when you've just broken a radiator hose and your car has arrived at the garage on the back of a tow truck.)

Another reason a shop manager might turn down your request for a specific mechanic might be the fact that the man you asked for (or the woman, as is entirely possible nowadays) does not specialize in the type of work you want done. A dealer or independent garage is likely to employ a transmission specialist, a tuneup expert, and other helpers individually adept at dealing with electrical, fuel, and front-end problems. In smaller shops, of course, there'll be some doubling up of these responsibilities. But if you want a tuneup and you ask for the transmission man, the manager is naturally going to turn you down. It's just as well — you wouldn't want the manicurist cutting your hair, either.

Flat Rate: Not So Bad After All

Next to the quality of the work a garage does, your biggest question will probably have to do with how much, and how, you are going to be charged for it. This brings us to the pros and cons of flat rate, which have been bandied around probably as long as there have been cars to fix. A lot of consumer advocates would like to see flat rate abolished altogether — but, as we'll see, there really might not be any better replacement for it.

What exactly is flat rate? Basically, it's the practice of charging for hourly labor on a repair job not on the basis of the actual time spent doing the job, but according to a "book estimate" of how long the job ought to take. Mechanics who charge flat rate use one or the other of the two comprehensive industry manuals, Motor's or Chilton's, which gives them the time estimates for just about every repair or replacement job that could possibly come along. (Both books, by the way, give identical estimates.) The two companies arrive at their figures by using the manufacturers' own estimates and adding 20 to 30 percent to the time involved. Why the addition? It's simple: when the manufacturer calculates repair times, he does it by assigning a particular job to a mechanic and timing his complete performance. This is done three times, and the average time is taken. But the manufacturer's mechanic is working on a brand-new car, with no frozen, rusted, or undercoated bolts and no blanket of grime on the engine. He also has every tool he needs at his fingertips and doesn't have to spend any preliminary diagnostic time on the job. So, when Motor's and Chilton's offer these estimates to their mechanic clientele, they adjust them to reflect the added difficulties likely to be encountered in the field.

(The original flat rate, by the way, still holds when it comes time for the manufacturers to reimburse dealers for work they have done on cars still under warranty. Some observers suspect that this is why dealers tend to assign warranty work to the junior mechanics in the shop, leaving the more experienced personnel available to work on jobs for which the book estimate will be paid.)

By now, you've probably guessed the universal complaint against flat rate. Why, people argue, should you have to pay a mechanic for time he may very well not have spent working on your car? After all, if everything goes right, a job estimated by Chilton's or Motor's (and, beneath the added-on percentage by the manufacturer) to take three hours might be completed by a competent mechanic in two or two and a half. Is something unfair going on?

Not really. Four advantages of flat rate come immediately to mind. First, you'll always know that a particular job is going to cost the same amount of money, as long as labor rates remain constant (of course, this is exclusive of the price of parts, which is always liable to escalation by the manufacturer). Second, flat rate enables a shop to write you an estimate and stay within it. Third, you'll know from the start how long the job is going to take and when to come back and pick up the car. Finally, you're assured that the price you were quoted is going to hold, even if your job presents special problems, such as frozen or broken bolts, that hold it up past the estimated time. The exception is when things are going so badly that the shop manager has to call you up and tell you that the job involves more work than either of you originally bargained for, and that extra time will be required. This is something he is obliged to do and that we'll talk about later.

Of course, no system is perfect, and there are ways in which a greedy garage keeper can turn flat rate to his unfair advantage. One is by rushing jobs so that he and his helpers get the times down to a smaller and smaller fraction of the book estimates. Theoretically this is fine — as long as the finished product is equal in quality to a job that would have taken longer. But as we all know, the odds against that kind of consistent result diminish as the race against the clock speeds up. And what happens when faulty jobs bounce back? They have to be redone in order for the shop to make good on its warranty. Ideally, the manager should hand the job back to the mechanic who did it in the first place and make him do it right. But in the real world, the kind of unscrupulous manager who encourages speed-demon work at flat rate is likely to pass "bounce" jobs on to his lower-echelon, minimum-wage employees. Teaching you to steer clear of this type of operation is one of the purposes of this book.

And don't forget: a shady shop owner can turn straight-hourly billing to his advantage as well, as can a lazy or lackadaisical character or even a mechanic who just doesn't happen to be feeling well on a particular day. If you're paying a straight-hourly rate — based solely on how long it takes to do your job and not on what the book says — and the mechanic has to answer three phone calls or decides to take a few coffee breaks, you're paying for his distractions and procrastination. If you're paying flat rate, the price quoted has to be the price charged, even if he takes ten coffee breaks and talks on the phone for an hour. With flat rate, the mechanic pays for his own idling.

There isn't much in modern life that we don't pay flat rate for. The barber has a fixed charge for a haircut or a shampoo. The dentist charges so much for a filling, so much for a cap, and so much for a root-canal job. So it shouldn't seem odd, or necessarily dishonest, for a mechanic to consult his Chilton's manual and base his charge on the book estimate when you come in to have your MacPherson struts replaced.

Closely related to the question of flat rate is what we call the "menu job." That's when a garage, in its advertisements or on-premises signboards, offers a certain job at a set price. These are the common jobs that everyone needs from time to time, such as replacement of brake shoes or disc-brake pads, tuneups, wheel alignments, and the like. The sign or ad will tell you just what work will be performed for the set price — for instance, a disc-brake job will consist of removing the calipers, putting the new pads in, and putting the calipers back on. If it turns out that the discs have to be ground down, or if you want extra services such as wheel-bearing repacking, you'll receive additional billing at the prevailing flat rate for these jobs. There's nothing at all wrong with a menu job, as long as you clearly understand what's on the menu and what you'll have to pay for it. If it's a tuneup, it should be clear just what filters are to be replaced and what adjustments checked and corrected. Spark plugs and (if you

don't have electronic ignition) points are also on that particular menu, with the price varying according to how many cylinders your car's engine has. All in all, buying off the menu is a good way to take care of things such as routine checkups.

Don't confuse a menu job with the purchase of a rebuilt unit, such as a transmission. Sure, there's a set price for purchase and installation, but you don't know just which components of the trans were replaced and which are original. Even if there's a guarantee, you still have no idea what you're getting.

Writing the Repair Order

The repair order, or "RO" as we'll call it here, is the first important key to getting a satisfactory job done on your car. Nothing could be simpler, but nothing can cause more havoc later on if it isn't taken care of properly at the start.

Repair orders serve a number of important purposes. They describe what has to be done on the car, and when signed by the customer, they constitute the contract authorizing the mechanic to

Towing

When your car won't run, you have to decide on the spot what to do with it. Can it be repaired where it is, or must it be removed to a garage?

Moving a disabled car can be a problem, especially if you try to do it yourself. It is difficult to move the car safely by what is called a "flat tow," which involves another vehicle and a tow rope or chain. The hookup from car to car must

be made under the car to a good chassis tow-point, because bumpers on most cars today are either soft-plastic-faced or are of the 5-mile-per-hour-collapsible-crash type. Either of these will be damaged if a tow hookup is attempted.

The same is true should you attempt to push a car. There are no bumper guards or bumper over-rides (vertical parts) to prevent one car from riding over the other's bumper and causing body damage.

The best way to move a disabled car is to call a reputable tow company and let them assume all of the responsibility. Remember one additional point if you do get the car moving on your own: most cars today are equipped with power steering and power brakes. Without the engine running, there will be no power for the brakes, and no steering assist.

proceed with repairs. In fact, many states have consumer laws stipulating that an individual need not pay for services performed unless he or she has authorized those services by signing a repair order. The repair order is also a valuable part of your records of ownership and maintenance, as we'll discuss later on.

The first thing you want to do when it comes time for describing your car's problems and writing up the repair order is to establish the fact that you are genuinely interested in the matter at hand and want it explained to you in terms that you can understand. A lot of us have had our experiences with the patronizing, don't-worry-I'll-take-care-of-it attitude some mechanics have — an attitude that is best nipped in the bud by a polite yet firm assertion that you wish to be treated as a knowledgeable adult (although you shouldn't say it in so many words).

Once that relationship has been established, you want to get down to some obvious yet often overlooked repair-order specifics. These include your name,

An estimate and repair order describes what has to be done on a car, and, when signed by the customer, constitutes the contract authorizing the mechanic to proceed with repairs and costs specified — and no more.

address, home phone, *and the number of a phone at which you can be reached during the day*. This last item cannot be emphasized too strongly: if the mechanic has no way of reaching you during the day, an unexpected hitch in the repair job could lead to one or both of a pair of unpleasant surprises. You might find out that you're in for more than you originally thought you had to pay, or you might end up standing around at the garage with no ride home and your car still up on the rack. Now, we've already mentioned that in many states, you don't have to pay for what you haven't agreed to in writing, no more than you have to pay for something that comes in the mail when you haven't ordered it. But let's be fair. If the mechanic has no way of reaching you, and something needs to be done with your car that you haven't originally discussed or signed for, he has to come to a quick decision as to what to do with a large and very likely immobile piece of your property that is cluttering up his premises. The logical thing is to fix it, get it out of the way, and get on with the other work that pays his rent. Why not avoid this quandary simply by leaving word as to where you're going to be? If that's impossible, at least try to check back once or twice during the day.

Next, make sure that the year, make, and model of the car appear correctly on the RO, and that the *mileage* and *date* are written down. Mileage and date verify the terms of the warranty; it's not unusual for cases involving repair warranties to be thrown out of small-claims court because these items were neglected. Even if there's never any problem with warranties or litigation, it's still handy to have a record of the dates and mileage at which specific checkups and repairs were made, both for your own satisfaction and as proof of maintenance should the need for it ever arise. (One example of such need might be a theft-insurance claim. If your car is stolen, and the insurance company wants to depreciate its value on the basis of lack of maintenance, a complete repair-order file can prove that the car was kept in good condition.)

Manufacturers' policies on replacement of parts during new-car warranty periods provide another good reason for keeping an up-to-date file of your repair orders. Most manufacturers will extend the warranty for the particular part that's been replaced: if you've got a 12,000-mile warranty, and the transmission is replaced at 9,000 miles, they'll stand behind the replacement unit for the first 12,000 miles of *its* life, even though that will bring total car mileage up to 21,000. The proof that this kind of warranty stands on is the 9,000-mile figure, written at the head of the RO tucked safely in your files.

We can't overemphasize the importance of following the repair-order procedure to the letter. However handy your personal log might be, it can never stand up as a legal document. In fact, a number of states regard the RO as such an important part of the car-repair transaction that customers are not legally obliged to pay for any work not represented on orders that they — the customers — have not signed.

Describing What's Wrong with Your Car

Describing a problem with an automobile can itself be a problem, one of the most difficult that the mechanic and the consumer have to face. What is a skip? A miss? A rumble? A rattle? A vibration? You've got to be specific about *what* the car is doing, *when* it does it, and *how* it is affecting performance, drivability, or whatever. These may seem like simple, stock questions, but the answers don't always come so easily. Ideally, the service manager should help things along by doing some asking as well as just listening. He might ask, for instance, just what it was that the car did that you didn't think it was supposed to do, whether it occurs at a particular time or place or under certain conditions, and how long you have noticed the problem. Be prepared to answer as specifically as possible; a few thoughtful minutes here can save wasted diagnostic time later. One question will lead to another, and before long the mechanic may have a pretty good idea of just what the problem is. Or, at least he'll have it reasonably narrowed down.

One thing you want to watch out for is a mechanic who seems to have the answer before he even asks any questions. If you walk into the garage and say, "My car doesn't start well," and the service man says, "Well, you probably need a tuneup," without waiting to hear the details, a warning flag should go up. There are a lot of things that can cause hard starting, and a tuneup may not get to the bottom of any of them. "When doesn't it start?" the mechanic should ask. "When it's hot? When it's on a hill? When it's cold?" Your answers will guide him in the right direction.

But if the mechanic shouldn't jump to conclusions, then neither should you. One of the biggest mistakes you can make when you go to a garage is to walk in with the diagnosis of your problem all neatly wrapped up and ready to deliver to the mechanic. Maybe you have an acquaintance whose car had symptoms similar to yours, and your conclusion is that what worked for him will work for you. That conclusion may be wrong — and your misplaced confidence in it can send the mechanic off on the wrong track. It's always better to describe the problem as clearly as possible, answer questions thoroughly, and let the mechanic make an objective evaluation of what's wrong.

Now, the key word in that last sentence is *clearly*. Like every other field of technical endeavor, auto maintenance has its own vocabulary, its own shorthand language for describing certain objects, pro-

cesses, and situations. Obviously, a layman can't be expected to master every term having to do with cars and the problems they develop. But it doesn't take much trouble to learn the basics and to acquire a habit for precision in describing mechanical symptoms. In part, that is the purpose of the "troubleshooting" chapter later in this book — to acquaint you with some common problems and the language used to convey them to professionals.

Here's an example of how a poor grasp of automotive vocabulary led to more than simple confusion over a particular problem. A man went to a garage and told the mechanic that his car was "dieseling." This is a condition in which the engine continues to run after the ignition switch has been turned off; it's caused by a carburetor maladjustment that allows air and fuel vapors to enter the combustion chamber, where they are ignited by heat remaining in the chamber. The mechanic checked the carburetor, made whatever adjustment seemed necessary, and sent his customer off with an assurance that everything should be all right. But everything wasn't. When the problem the customer called dieseling turned out to have been unaffected by the mechanic's work, he returned to the garage, somewhat annoyed, and asked the mechanic to come along on a drive so he could hear the problem firsthand. This struck him as odd, since you don't have to move a car an inch to tell whether or not the motor runs on after you turn it off.

The mechanic wasn't puzzled for long. About halfway up a hill, the car's engine went into a spark knock condition, at which point the customer said, "Do you hear it? It's dieseling." To him, *dieseling* meant the engine sounded more like a diesel than a gasoline engine — not an unreasonable idea, but one at odds with the definition of the word universally accepted among professional mechanics. His error in terminology was compounded by the mechanic's mistake in not asking pointed questions when the customer first came in.

In the end, though, they did what a customer and mechanic should always do when the description of symptoms is elusive or unclear: they took the car out for a test drive. That's part of the job, and the customer should be happy to pay for it.

Unless you have asked for a specific job — say, something off the menu — the repair order should not be written in terms of a specific job or jobs. It should be written to describe the findings of the road tester or the problems known to exist with the car. In short, the *symptoms* should appear on the RO. If they do not, you might have a hard time proving later that those were the symptoms you originally described and wanted corrected. If you want on-the-spot proof that the problems have been taken care of, just ask to be taken out for a short demonstration ride. If the symptoms persist, it will be an easy matter to refer right back to the description on the RO and request that the job be done over.

There are three basic reasons why a car is brought into a garage, and the one that applies in each individual case should be reflected in the writeup on the RO. The first reason is the most obvious one: something isn't working right. The second is that the car is going to be taken on a long trip, and the owner wants to make sure that everything is in good, dependable working order. The third is that it's time for a prescribed checkup.

We've already talked about the first reason for taking the car to the shop and how the problems should be written up. As for the second reason, the RO should state: "Get car ready for trip." It may also refer to specific menu jobs commonly associated with preparations for long-distance travel, such as tuneup, wheel-bearing repack, and front-end alignment. This leaves the third reason for visiting your mechanic: the routine checkup.

When a car comes in for routine maintenance, the repair order should either specifically list the replacements, adjustments, and inspections that are to be performed, or should refer to the appropriate instructions in the owner's manual. If the RO says "as per manufacturer's specifications for 12,000-mile checkup," both the customer and the mechanic doing the work will know exactly which operations are required. The RO shouldn't be vague on this subject, and the customer should not assume too much. When your dealer's service manager calls you in for a routine visit, you're certainly within your rights to ask him just what is entailed and to see it on paper. Also, compare his description of the checkup with the prescribed procedures in the owner's manual to see that everything is accounted for.

Estimates: What Are Your Rights?

The price of repairs should always be estimated before the work is done. In most states, consumer law obligates the garage to keep the final price to within 10 percent of the original estimate, *unless* the customer has been contacted and told of additional charges before the work proceeds and those charges are incurred. (Remember a few pages back, when we talked about how important it is to leave both regular and alternate phone numbers with the garage when the repair order is written?) If the customer can't be reached, the law technically has it that he or she is not liable for charges in excess of the estimate plus 10 percent.

This sounds fine on paper. But in practical terms, it's usually the best policy to avoid an unpleasant altercation at the garage by paying the bill and then taking your case to small-claims court for reimbursement. (If you follow this route, of course, you'll also want to look for another mechanic — but if your gripe against the first one is strong enough to send you into litigation, you'll want to end your dealings with him anyway.) It's a good idea, though, to try to think beyond the two-dimensional legalities and temper your reaction to unanticipated yet justifiable repair charges on the basis of your past relationship with the mechanic, the quality of the work he has done for you, and the good faith he may have shown in trying to reach you before going ahead with the work. He may honestly have assumed that you would have said, "Yes, go ahead," and perhaps he would have been right. Both sides should play by the rules at first; but once you've felt each other out and established some trust, don't be so quick to run into court unless that trust has been clearly violated. And if you absolutely do not want the mechanic to proceed beyond the original estimate, then say so at the beginning and get it in writing on the repair order.

The Value of a Second Opinion

If you haven't yet developed a solid, trusting relationship with one garage, or if a job is particularly complicated and expensive, you may wish to seek a second opinion as to the nature of your car's problem, the recommended solution, and the cost. Looking for another professional's corroboration of an initial diagnosis makes just as much sense in the world of car repairs as it does in medicine and surgery. And just as you must expect to pay consultation fees for second and third opinions from medical doctors, so too should you plan on paying mechanics for diagnoses and estimates on your car. The amount a garage will charge for making a repair estimate will reflect that garage's hourly rate, the regular flat rate for procedures such as hookups to electronic diagnostic machinery, and the price of materials used.

What happens if the second opinion you receive differs substantially from the first? You go for a third. And if that third visit results in yet another dissenting opinion, you owe it to yourself to keep shopping around until a single approach to the problem has been reasonably corroborated. It isn't often that you'll be led on such a merry chase, but if you are, just consider the time spent an investment in your peace of mind.

Checking the Bill and Evaluating the Job

Now the job is done. You're back at the garage to pick up your car and pay the bill. But you don't just take out your checkbook, settle up, and say goodbye. First, go over the bill with the service manager and have him explain each of the itemized parts to you. Never be satisfied with a bill on which the parts are listed only by number; you should be sure of the name of each part and how it was related to the job that was done.

Next, check to make sure that the total price for the job came to within 10 percent of the initial estimate — as we noted before, that's the legal cutoff in many states.

Was the job done within the amount of time originally estimated, barring delays explained to you as they occurred? It's fair to expect that unless you have been so notified, the car will be ready for you to pick up at the time promised. Watch out for any garage that establishes a pattern of making unrealistic promises as to how long jobs will take — with that kind of shop, the idea is to lure you in, get you to sign for the job, and then hit you later with the news that the car will be in longer than was originally figured. Some states have laws stipulating that unless you are notified at the start that a job will involve keeping the car overnight, the garage is responsible for providing you with transportation if the job isn't finished at the end of the day.

The next step in checking the job can get a little clumsy — you might even get grease on your hands — but it is important. You have to ask the mechanic to give you the old parts he took out of your car. Not show them to you, but give them to you. They're yours, and you have a right to them. There's no other way to make sure that those parts were indeed replaced and not just doctored up, cleaned, and passed off as new. The exception is when you've agreed to pay for a rebuilt rather than a new part. In that situation, the garage has to send the replaced unit to the shop that does the rebuilding so that he may receive his "core" charge and the old part from your car may itself be rebuilt. Still, you have the right to see the removed part before it gets sent out.

If you are paying for a new part, don't let the garage keeper keep the old one and send it in for rebuilding. If anyone should get credit on that part with the rebuilder, it should be you.

What do you do with those greasy pieces of junk that you've asked the mechanic to give you? Throw them away, far from the garage, so that there is no chance they'll be recycled as bogus parts "removed" from some future customer's car. Some of the better shops will even give you a plastic bag to cart them away in.

Sometimes, it will be impractical for you to ask for and carry off everything that was removed. A muffler and tailpipe assembly, for example, can be left at the garage. Just make sure you've seen it and that you've taken a look at what will be obviously identifiable as a new muffler/tailpipe underneath your car.

As Time Goes By: Maintaining Trust Is a Two-Way Street

Keeping up a good working relationship with your regular garage and mechanic is well worth the little bit of effort required on both sides. For your part, remember that there's a lot to be lost by becoming a "floater" who constantly shops around for the cheapest price; that's not the main purpose of seeking second opinions. Find a good shop, and stick with it. You'll save money and time in the long run.

This doesn't mean that there's any special stigma attached to doing as much as you can of your own work. Most garage owners respect that initiative, perhaps in part because it provides them with a certain amount of Monday morning business when the less successful weekend do-it-yourselfers come in. Do your own repairs

if you wish, but *don't* buy parts in the store and bring them to the garage expecting the mechanic to install them. This is every bit as taboo as bringing your own food to a restaurant and expecting the chef to cook it for you. Part of the garage's profit is justifiably based on new-parts markup; if he were denied this income, the owner would have to charge a much higher hourly labor rate.

The garage owner has to keep up his end of the deal as well, and it makes good sense to keep a friendly eye on his track record for high-quality workmanship and business ethics. If you keep your repair-order file up to date, you'll be able to tell if you're being called in for checkups or repairs that aren't necessary or that are being suggested for too frequent intervals.

The frequency of repairs may also tell you something about whether the quality of your mechanic's work is falling off. Take tuneups as an example. Depending on the car, a tuneup should last from 10,000 to 30,000 miles (on newer cars with electronic ignition, the intervals are at the longer end of the scale). If the car goes out of tune way too soon, you've got one of two problems: a defect in the car, or a defect in the mechanic. When the problem isn't solved on the first or second visit to the garage, it's probably the mechanic. And if his approach is one of simply yanking out parts and replacing them — a hit-and-miss game for which you can pay dearly — rather than taking a road test and making a reasoned diagnosis, it's time to do some "replacing" of your own.

That's the nature of the car-repair business. But what we've learned in this chapter is so much abstract theory if we don't also learn about the nature of the car. In the following chapters, we'll look at cars system-by-system so that you'll be able to speak the mechanic's language even when you can't make the repairs yourself.

WILLYS KNIGHT

LINCOLN

B

STANDARD

B
IX

Studebaker

CHEVROLET

De Soto

WI
K

dge

DODGEM

old

HYDRA-MATIC

What's Under the Hood?

Introduction to the Automobile

Almost all cars on the road today run on four wheels and somewhere in their bodies house an engine, transmission, differential, and a host of other accessories and systems needed to get from place to place.

It is the location of these components that makes today's cars confusing, since advances in technology and the quest for fuel economy have brought about departures from long-accepted norms. Time was when we could always be safe in the

Top View of Rear-Wheel-Drive Front-Mounted 4 Cylinder Gasoline Engine

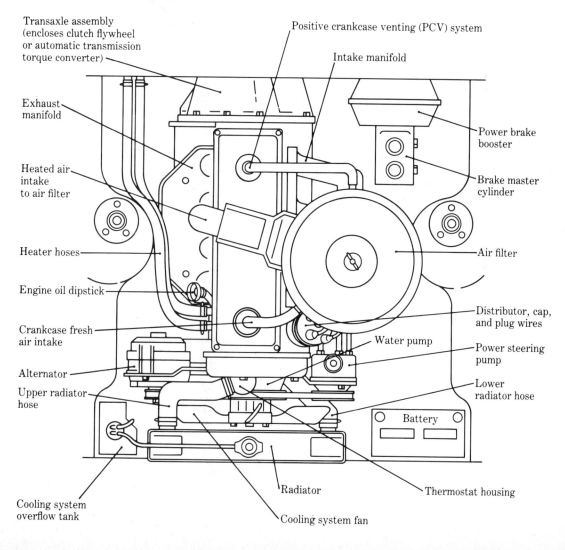

Transaxle assembly (encloses clutch flywheel or automatic transmission torque converter)

Positive crankcase venting (PCV) system

Intake manifold

Exhaust manifold

Power brake booster

Heated air intake to air filter

Brake master cylinder

Heater hoses

Air filter

Engine oil dipstick

Distributor, cap, and plug wires

Crankcase fresh air intake

Water pump

Power steering pump

Alternator

Upper radiator hose

Lower radiator hose

Battery

Cooling system overflow tank

Radiator

Cooling system fan

Thermostat housing

assumption that the engine would be in the front and that the rear wheels would be the ones to apply power to the ground to make the car move. Now we can't be so sure, and no single diagram, photo, or description of an engine or drive train could possibly serve the entire gamut of car designs.

In this chapter we will attempt to identify major components and their locations through the use of several composite illustrations that will show the placement of the engine on both front-wheel-drive and rear-wheel-drive cars and identify the engine's mounting position and direction. The illustrations will also identify the components found in the front-wheel and rear-

Top View of Front-Wheel-Drive Transverse-Mounted 4 Cylinder Gasoline Engine

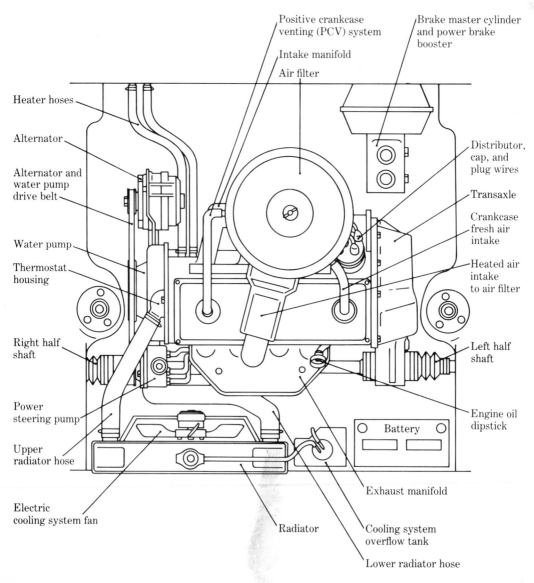

Positive crankcase venting (PCV) system

Brake master cylinder and power brake booster

Intake manifold

Air filter

Heater hoses

Alternator

Alternator and water pump drive belt

Water pump

Thermostat housing

Right half shaft

Power steering pump

Upper radiator hose

Electric cooling system fan

Distributor, cap, and plug wires

Transaxle

Crankcase fresh air intake

Heated air intake to air filter

Left half shaft

Engine oil dipstick

Battery

Exhaust manifold

Radiator

Cooling system overflow tank

Lower radiator hose

wheel-drive lines. For many, it will be the
first experience under a car.

The following illustrations are of
the most common systems in general use
today. There are others, however, and
just as always, man has found a way to
foul up the order of things by inventing
the unusual.

Top View of Front-Wheel-Drive Longitudinally-Mounted 4 Cylinder Gasoline Engine

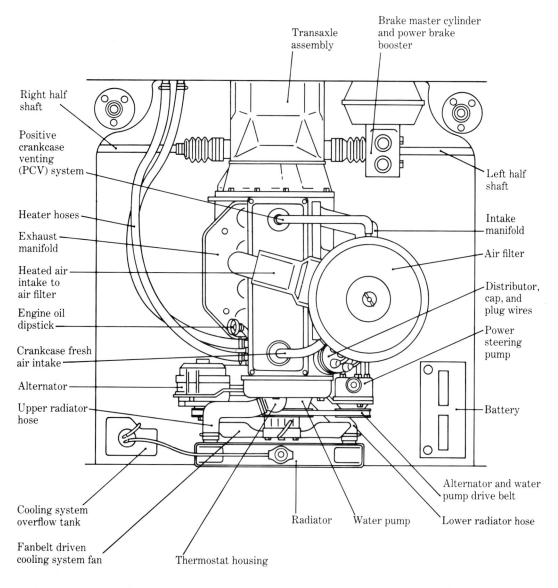

Rear-Wheel-Drive, Front-Mounted Engine Chassis (Passenger Cars and Light Trucks)

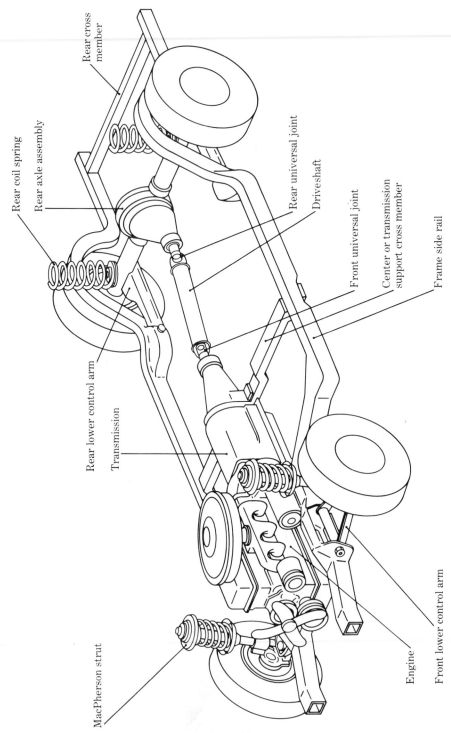

Rear cross member

Rear coil spring

Rear axle assembly

Rear universal joint

Driveshaft

Front universal joint

Center or transmission support cross member

Frame side rail

Rear lower control arm

Transmission

MacPherson strut

Engine

Front lower control arm

Front-Wheel-Drive, Transverse Front-Mounted Engine Chassis (Passenger Cars and Light Trucks)

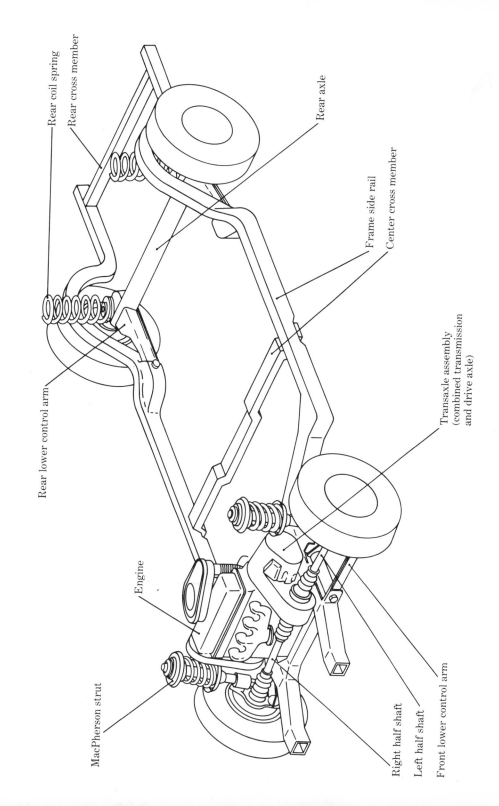

Rear coil spring

Rear cross member

Rear axle

Frame side rail

Center cross member

Rear lower control arm

Transaxle assembly (combined transmission and drive axle)

Engine

MacPherson strut

Right half shaft

Left half shaft

Front lower control arm

Front-Wheel-Drive, Longitudinally-Mounted Engine Chassis (Passenger Cars)

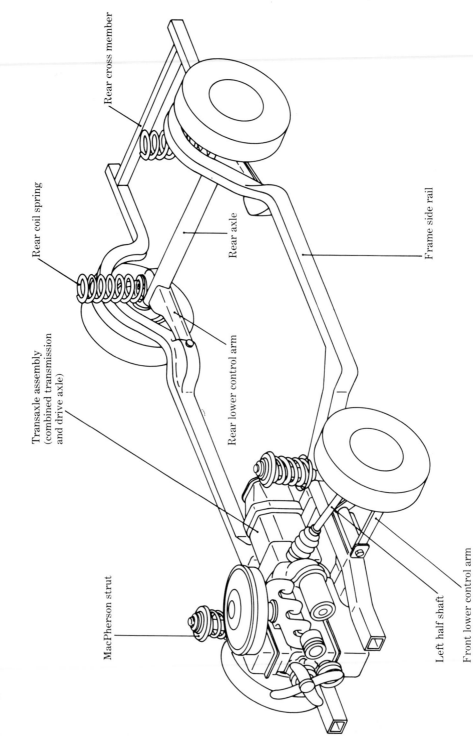

Rear cross member

Rear coil spring

Rear axle

Frame side rail

Transaxle assembly (combined transmission and drive axle)

Rear lower control arm

MacPherson strut

Left half shaft

Front lower control arm

Rear-Wheel-Drive, Transverse Mid-Engine Chassis (Two Seat Sports Cars)

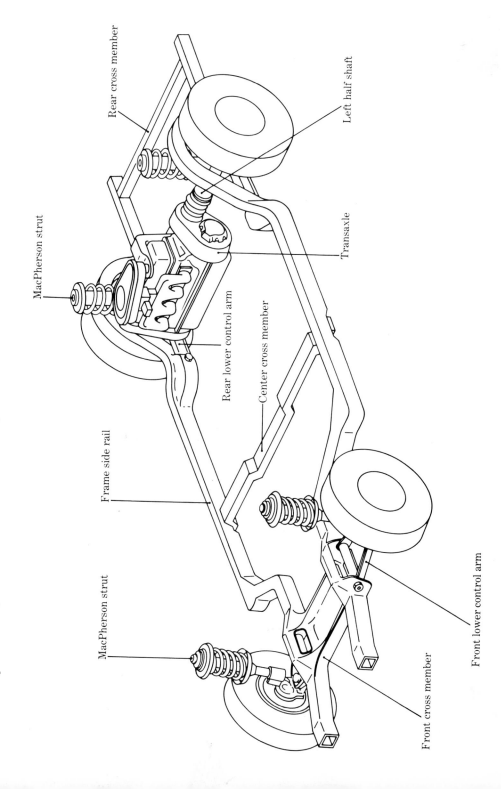

Rear cross member

Left half shaft

MacPherson strut

Transaxle

Rear lower control arm

Center cross member

Frame side rail

MacPherson strut

Front cross member

Front lower control arm

Four-Wheel-Drive Chassis (Utility Vehicles)

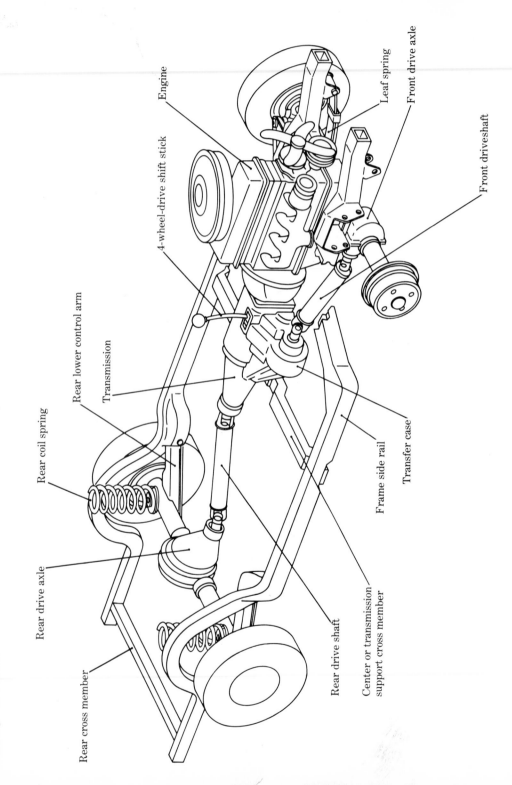

Engine

Leaf spring

Front drive axle

4-wheel-drive shift stick

Front driveshaft

Rear lower control arm

Transmission

Rear coil spring

Transfer case

Frame side rail

Rear drive axle

Rear cross member

Rear drive shaft

Center or transmission support cross member

The Dual Hydraulic Front-to-Rear Brake System

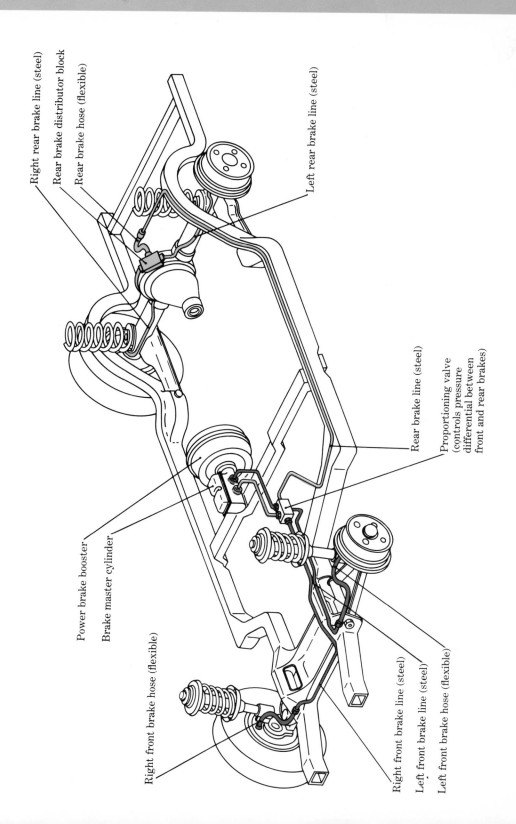

Right rear brake line (steel)

Rear brake distributor block

Rear brake hose (flexible)

Left rear brake line (steel)

Rear brake line (steel)

Proportioning valve (controls pressure differential between front and rear brakes)

Power brake booster

Brake master cylinder

Right front brake hose (flexible)

Right front brake line (steel)

Left front brake line (steel)

Left front brake hose (flexible)

A Typical Cooling System

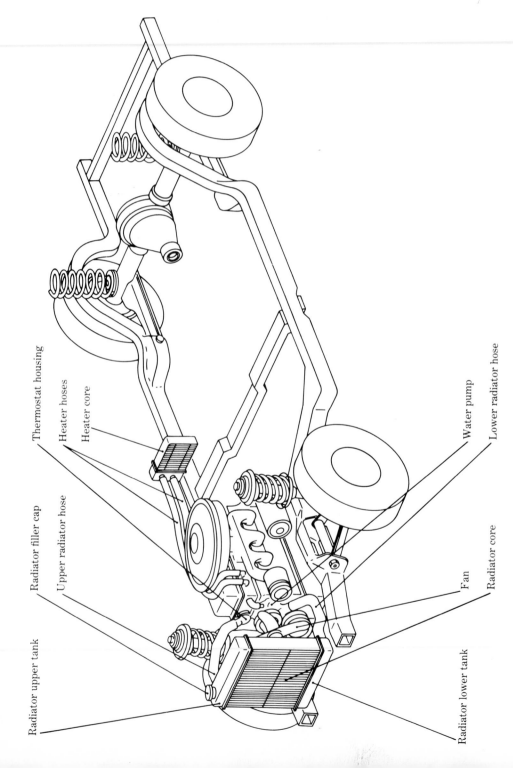

Radiator upper tank

Radiator filler cap

Upper radiator hose

Thermostat housing

Heater hoses

Heater core

Water pump

Lower radiator hose

Fan

Radiator core

Radiator lower tank

A Typical Fuel System

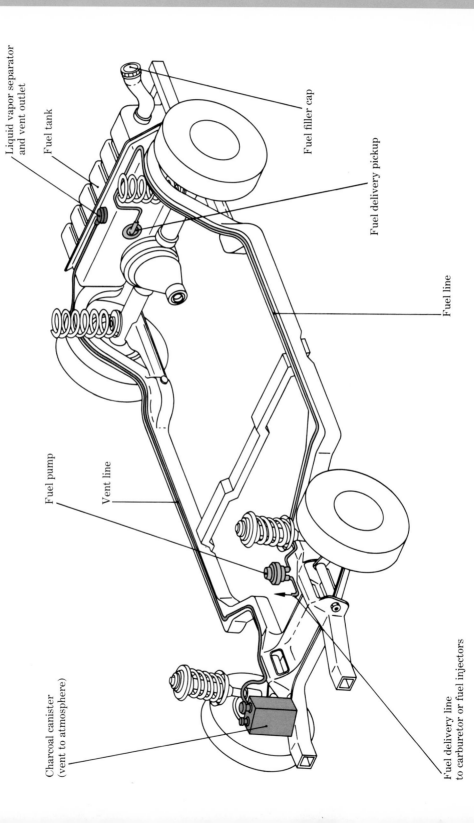

Liquid vapor separator
and vent outlet

Fuel tank

Fuel filler cap

Fuel delivery pickup

Fuel line

Fuel pump

Vent line

Charcoal canister
(vent to atmosphere)

Fuel delivery line
to carburetor or fuel injectors

The Electrical System and How It Works

The internal-combustion engine does not run on gasoline alone. It takes electricity, which, translated into motion, gets the engine to turn before it can fire; and into a high-voltage spark, ignites the air-fuel mixture in the cylinders. Thus the *electrical system* is a vital part of every automobile.

We can divide the car's electrical workings into four subsystems, each with its own job to do. The *starting system* takes voltage and amperage from the battery and converts it to rotary motion to get the engine to turn over, or "spin," when we turn the ignition switch to

"start." The *ignition system* takes voltage from the battery and steps it up to produce the spark needed for combustion. The *accessory system* comprises the radio, heater, air conditioner, windshield wipers, rear-window defroster, power windows and seats, and other essential and optional equipment (see chapter 9), all of which draw energy from the battery or from the charging system to operate. The *charging system* uses the rotary motion of the engine to produce electricity to recharge the battery.

The Starting System

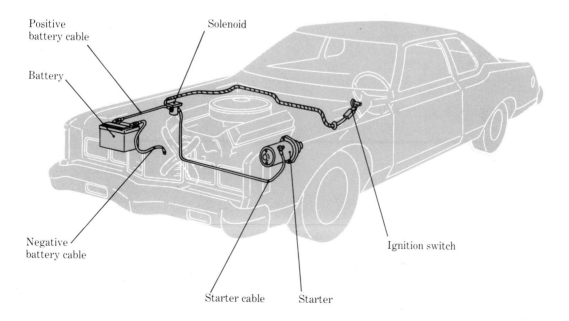

Positive battery cable

Solenoid

Battery

Negative battery cable

Ignition switch

Starter cable

Starter

The Ignition System

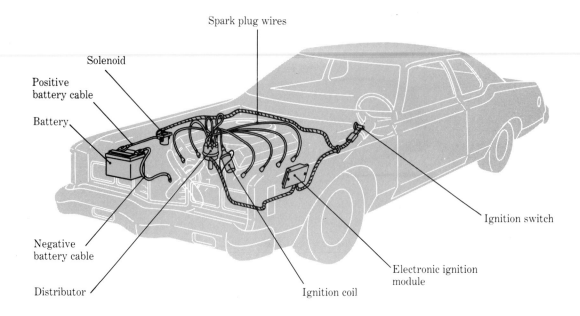

Spark plug wires

Solenoid

Positive
battery cable

Battery

Negative
battery cable

Distributor

Ignition coil

Electronic ignition
module

Ignition switch

The Charging System

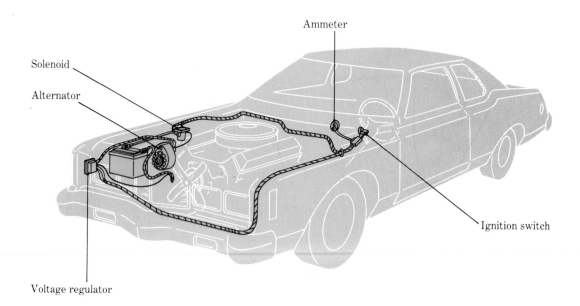

Ammeter

Solenoid

Alternator

Ignition switch

Voltage regulator

The Accessory System

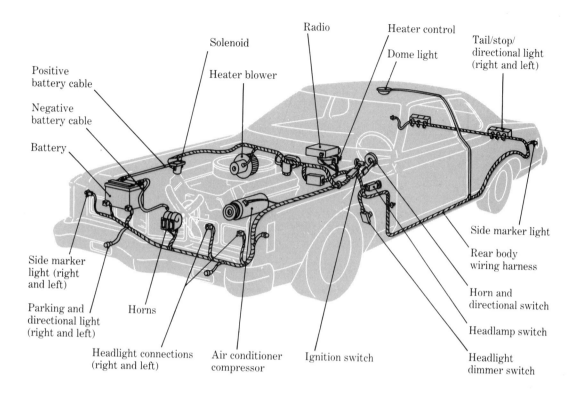

Radio

Heater control

Solenoid

Dome light

Tail/stop/
directional light
(right and left)

Heater blower

Positive
battery cable

Negative
battery cable

Battery

Side marker light

Rear body
wiring harness

Side marker
light (right
and left)

Horn and
directional switch

Parking and
directional light
(right and left)

Horns

Headlamp switch

Headlight connections
(right and left)

Air conditioner
compressor

Ignition switch

Headlight
dimmer switch

The Battery

As you can see, this brief review of the auto's electrical subsystems begins and ends with the battery. The battery in today's car is a lead-acid storage device. It is made up of a number of cells, each of which contains lead-alloy plates immersed in an electrolyte solution of sulfuric acid and water. A battery does not store electricity as electricity; it stores it in the form of a reversible chemical reaction between the plates and the electrolyte.

The two phases of this reversible reaction are called *discharge* and *charge*. When you turn the key in a car and energize the starter, current — a flow of electrons — begins to flow from the negative post of the battery and the discharge cycle begins. As it takes place, the electrolyte solution gives up sulfur to the lead plates,

and the solution itself more closely approaches the composition of ordinary water. (When a battery is completely dead, the electrolyte is mostly water.) During the charge cycle, which we'll look at in detail below, the sulfur disengages from the plates and goes back into solution with the electrolyte.

The more plates a battery has, the more *amperage* it is capable of putting out. Amperage is a measure of electric current; it represents the *volume* of electrons rushing through a circuit. *Voltage*, on the other hand, refers to the force, or pressure, behind the flow. An analogy with water in a pipe or hose is often used. If the tap is turned off, you've got pressure without having an actual flow. That corresponds to voltage. When the tap is turned on, you've got x gallons of water per minute surging through the pipe or hose, *with the pressure behind it*. Thus the comparison with volts and amperes, or amps.

There are several ways of rating car batteries. One universal method is by voltage, which is now a uniform 12 volts in the batteries of all cars sold in the United States. There was a time when some smaller cars had 6-volt batteries; the last of these, though, was the Volkswagen bug of the early 1970s. How do you tell a 6-volt from a 12-volt battery? It's simple — just count the number of caps on the top of the battery. Each cap indicates a separate cell, and each cell is capable of holding two volts. Thus a 6-volt battery has three caps, and a 12-volt battery has six.

Another battery-rating system is based on *ampere hours*. It tells us how many amps a battery will put out over one hour, or over the commonly used standard of twenty hours. The greater the number

of plates a battery has, the higher its ampere-hour rating.

The ampere-hour figure is a good way to rate batteries, but when you go into an auto-supply store to buy a battery, you may find that they are listed according to a different system, by *group number*. The group number simply refers to the dimensions of the outside case of the battery and does not usually give any indication of the quality of the battery or of the number of ampere hours it is capable of putting out.

Within each group-number classification, there will often be three or four levels of quality, most commonly expressed as differences in the duration of the warranty: 24, 36, 48, or even 60 months. Usually, the rule is that the longer a battery is warranted for, the higher its ampere-hour capacity. It's important to think in terms of that capacity and not simply expected duration of

The Battery

The case of most batteries is a single piece plastic tub containing six separate compartments into which plates are inserted. Straps known as cell connectors join the plates to the adjacent cell. The end cells are attached to the battery terminal (or post) through the case (or cover).

Filler cap

Top

Terminal (or post)

Case

Plates

Cell connector and plate strap

service. For example, you may be shopping for a battery for a car you only intend to keep for another year. Let's say your car requires a group-24 battery with an ampere-hour capacity of 45. In view of your plans to trade the car within the year, you may decide to buy a group-24 battery with only a 24-month warranty. But that battery may only have an ampere-hour capacity of 30 or 35, rather than the 45 that you need. What happens? On a cold morning, when the battery's power is only 20 to 30 percent of what it is at 70°F, your car probably won't start. The proper way to buy a battery, then, is to select from the right size group, *and* to consult your car owner's manual for the recommended ampere-hour rating, or "cold cranking power" rating. The rating of the battery you buy should be no less than what the manual tells you.

Once you've got the right battery in your automobile, you can make it last a lot longer by following some simple maintenance rules. Perhaps the most important is to keep the battery fully charged. There are a number of things that can keep a battery from maintaining a full charge. If the car doesn't start right, and you have to keep cranking the engine; if you have a slipping fan belt, or a faulty alternator or voltage regulator; or if you use the car for repeated short trips without keeping the engine running long enough to give the battery a good charge, it will remain in a state of partial discharge. If you leave it that way, the battery will become *sulfated*. Remember the back-and-forth chemical reaction, in which sulfur from the electrolyte is deposited upon and given up by the lead plates in the battery cells? When a battery becomes sulfated, the sulfur remains on those plates; it crystallizes and coats them so that the electrolyte can't get through and they become inactive.

A battery that has become sulfated has a peculiar way of acting. When you get into the car in the morning and turn the key, the engine will start — probably.

But should you stall the car and attempt to restart it, you'll find that the battery has gone dead. The reason the car won't start on this second try is that sulfation limits the capacity of the battery and thus the number of consecutive times it is available to restart the engine. A sulfated battery could also be responsible for your lights dimming when you come to a stop and let the engine idle; they'll brighten up again when you step on the gas.

If prolonged partial discharge of your battery is being caused by a mechanical problem — such as the above-mentioned slipping fan belt or faulty alternator — have the problem remedied as soon as possible. If short-haul driving and long stretches of not using the car are at fault, you might wish to invest in a device called a trickle charger. You simply plug the charger into a house outlet and connect it to the battery while the car is in the garage. The charger feeds a small amount of current into the battery and shuts off when full capacity is reached.

Other battery-maintenance steps include keeping the top and sides of the case clean, so that there is no buildup of fluffy white corrosive material. This can eat away at the metal tray that holds the battery, or at other adjacent surfaces of the car. Cleaning the battery case, terminals, and cable connections is simple. First of all, shut off the engine. (This applies to all battery maintenance and indeed to all under-hood work, except for certain troubleshooting procedures, adjustments to the carburetor, and specialized operations best left to a mechanic.) Mix up a paste of baking soda and water, and brush it onto the affected surfaces. (Use a paintbrush or old toothbrush for this job.) When the paste stops bubbling, wash it away with clean water and the corrosion will be gone.

Another reason to keep the top of the battery clean is to reduce the possibility of *self-discharge*. When a layer of salt, corrosion, and acid builds up on the surface of a battery, all that is needed is a little moisture for the whole top of the battery to become conductive, with electricity discharging from the positive to the negative terminal.

Once or twice a year, it's a good practice to loosen and remove the battery cables, clean them with the baking-soda solution inside and out, and perhaps brighten them with the special scraper/reamer sold for the purpose at auto shops. Reinstall them snugly, and add a thin coat of Vaseline to the battery terminal and surrounding cable connection. This will help keep corrosion from forming. By keeping the terminal contacts in good shape, you will decrease the possibility of self-discharge and failure of the engine to start.

The Charging System

Keeping the battery charged is the responsibility of the *charging system*. This is made up of the alternator, voltage regulator, fan belt (sometimes called the alternator belt), and associated wiring. The alternator is an electromechanical device, meaning that it takes rotary motion from the engine and converts it into electrical power, which can be fed back into the electrical system of the automobile.

When you are starting a car, or when the engine is idling, you're probably taking all the electrical current you need from the battery. But as the engine speed increases, and the alternator output increases along with it, a greater portion of the necessary electrical current is taken from the alternator, and a smaller portion is taken from the battery. Finally, at road speed, the battery is only receiving current rather than putting it out, and the alternator is not only charging the battery but is also supporting all of the other electrical requirements of the car. Here's where a slipping fan belt, or faulty alternator components such as diodes or brushes, can keep the battery and the car's electrical accessories from getting the full alternator output, resulting in the battery wearing down from shouldering too much of the load.

The voltage regulator does just that — it regulates the output voltage of the alternator so that the system does not overcharge. The normal charging voltage for today's automobile is between 13.8 and 15.3 volts. The alternator, if unregulated, would put out unlimited amounts of voltage at its rated amperage. This could ruin the battery and cause other electrical components of the car to burn out. The regulator does its job by reading both the output of the alternator and the level of charge of the battery. It then adjusts the alternator output accordingly and keeps it in the optimal voltage range quoted above.

It's important to remember that in spite of its function as a source of electricity for the car, an alternator needs a con-

Self-Starter

Could Ben Franklin ever have envisioned our modern system of personal transportation on that fateful kite-flying day? Without Franklin, Edison, Volta (Voltaic cell battery), and others involved in the early harnessing of electricity, the car would be sitting like a useless lump of metal by the side of the road.

It was the harnessing of electricity that made possible the development of the self-starter. Perhaps no other single device made driving so accessible to everyone. Prior to this invention, the infernal machine could be started only one way — get out and crank — but with electricity, the self-starter, and the Voltaic cell battery, anyone could press a switch and bring even the biggest engine to life.

stant *input* of voltage and current — in other words, it needs a charged battery as part of the system.

It's simple for the handy do-it-yourselfer to test an alternator-regulator system. For a test, the *field wire* (normally connected to the ignition system, bringing current to the alternator) is disconnected from the alternator and connected directly to the battery to bring full battery voltage to the alternator, bypassing the regulator. When this is done, the alternator puts out its full charge, which can be read by connecting a voltmeter across the battery. If the voltmeter reading indicates less than full charge, the alternator is at fault. If the charge is full, but the system hasn't been properly charging the battery under normal circumstances (i.e., when the regulator is included in the circuit), then the regulator is the faulty component. Replacing either the alternator or the regulator is not a difficult task.

The Ignition System

The ignition system boosts the 12 volts produced by the battery or the alternator to as high as 50,000 volts — voltage needed to jump the gaps on the spark plugs and ignite the air-fuel mixture in the combustion chambers. The system also has to time these sparks to occur at the proper instant, so that the fuel in the combustion chambers burns exactly when it is supposed to.

In cars built prior to the mid-1970s, the business end of the ignition system is comprised of *ignition breaker points* (usually referred to simply as "points") in the distributor; a *condenser*, also in the dis-

Mechanics use big volt/ohmmeters like this to test the alternator's electrical output and the ability of the regulator to pass that charge on to the battery. It's simple for handy do-it-yourselfers to test their own alternator-regulator systems on this or more modest equipment.

The Point Ignition System

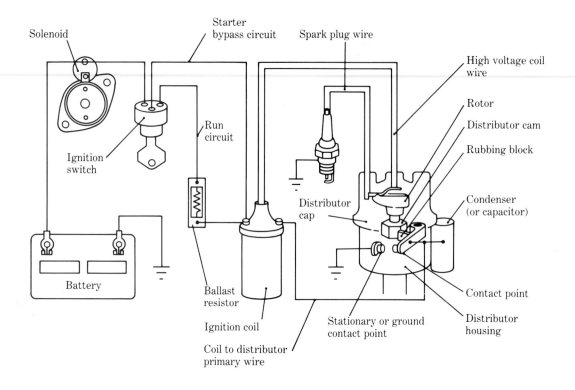

The Electronic Ignition System

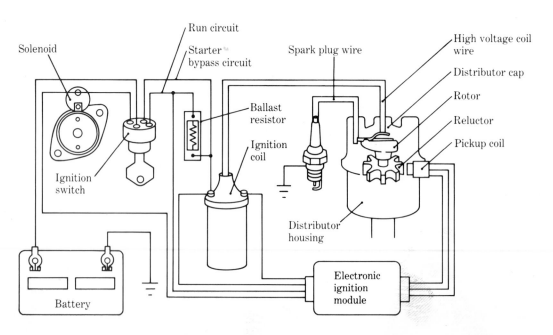

tributor; a *rotor cam*, mechanically driven by the engine to time the opening and closing of the points; a *rotor* and a *distributor cap* to distribute the high-voltage spark to the proper spark plugs; *spark plug wires* to connect the distributor cap to the spark plugs; and finally the *spark plugs* themselves, located in the combustion chambers in each cylinder of the engine.

Behind all this spark-delivery apparatus is the *ignition coil*. The ignition coil is a transformer that boosts the 12-volt electrical-system output to the high voltage needed for ignition. The coil has a primary winding and a secondary winding. The primary winding is connected to the points and ignition switch. When the ignition switch is turned on, current goes from the switch, through the primary winding, to the points. If the points are closed, current then flows through ground, creating a magnetic field in the primary winding of the ignition coil. When the turning of the rotor cam brings the points to an open position, the flow of electricity from the ignition switch through the primary winding is halted. This causes the magnetic

field in the coil to collapse. As the field collapses, it cuts across the secondary, or high-voltage, winding in the coil. This induces a high voltage in that winding. The high-voltage current is then sent out through the center tower of the coil to the center of the distributor cap and down through the cap to the rotor button, which is located at the top of the distributor shaft (the shaft is turning at one-half the engine speed). As the rotor turns, the point of the rotor points to the proper spark plug terminal in the distributor cap. The high-voltage current flows across the rotor gap to the spark plug terminal, through the plug wire to the spark, to fire the engine. When the rotor and shaft turn a bit more, the points close. This causes the magnetic field to build up in the coil once again, and the process is repeated.

In any 12-volt ignition system with points, there is a *resistor* between the coil and the ignition switch. This device limits the amount of amperage that can get through the coil to the points. When the resistor burns out, the car will only run when the ignition key is in the "start" position — when you crank the engine, it

Emergency Starting

One fine morning you'll want to start your car and the battery will be dead. The solution to your problem is booster cables, connected to a healthy car. Not just any booster cables will do. The kind you find in a discount store for $4.99 do not have enough capacity and can easily overheat. Expect to pay about $25 for heavy-duty cables that can really get the job done.

Here's how to use booster cables safely and effectively. First, the car with the good battery should have its engine turned off. Take the positive cable (red clamp) and attach it to the positive post of the good battery. Next, attach the other end of this cable to the posi-

tive post of the dead battery. Now attach the negative cable (black clamp) to the negative post of the good battery, and connect the other end *not to the dead battery*, but securely to the engine block of the immobilized car. Don't clamp the negative lead onto the body or anywhere else where grounding might be insufficient. The engine block is best. Above all, don't connect the two negative battery posts. This last negative connection should be as far from the battery as possible to prevent sparks — if there are any — from igniting an explosion of hydrogen gas present on top of the battery. In any event, some sort of eye protection should always be worn when doing any battery servicing, beyond a

simple checking of the electrolyte level.

When all of the proper connections have been made, start the car with the good battery. Allow the car to run at a fast idle for a few minutes so that its charging system will put a small charge into the disabled battery. Then start the disabled car. Once its engine turns over, allow it to run for a minute or two to make sure it won't stall. Finally, disconnect the cables, starting with the ground connection on the engine block of the revived car. The rest of the connections may be broken in any order.

will start, but it will die as soon as you let go of the key. If the resistor were not in place, or if it were not holding back enough current, the points would burn and could be rendered completely useless in as little as 500 miles of driving.

Electronic Ignition Systems

Toward the middle of the 1970s, ignition in the internal-combustion engines used in our cars was revolutionized by the introduction of solid-state electronics. In an electronic ignition system, there are no points, only a "magic box" containing a series of transistors. A transistor is merely an on-off switch, which can be activated by an extremely low-voltage, low-amperage draw. In this application, the source of that draw is a pickup coil in the distributor, which replaces the old ignition points.

As the distributor shaft rotates, a magnet attached to the shaft passes the pickup coil; its position is what tells the transistors to turn on and off. When the transistors turn on, current flows through the primary side of the ignition coil, and ignition proceeds in very much the same fashion as was described above for the traditional system. When the magnet rotates farther, it shuts the transistor off. This causes the collapse of the magnetic field, the inducement of high voltage in the secondary winding, and the passage of that high-voltage current to the spark distribution network. Again, operation is much the same as with the point apparatus from here on in.

One of the principal benefits of electronic ignition is the absence of friction. In the old setup, there is a rubbing block on the points that is in constant physical contact with the rotor cam. It has to be; otherwise, the points would not be able to open and close mechanically on cue. But as the cam turns, the block wears — so a tuneup actually begins to deteriorate as soon as you start the car and drive out of the garage. In an electronic ignition system, however, there are no rubbing parts, which means the timing of the spark is

unaffected by incremental wear, and the tuneup will last a lot longer.

Service requirements for the electronic ignition system are minimal. In addition to there being no friction-related wear, there are no points to burn and very little that can go wrong inside the distributor. Most of the servicing for the system can be accomplished by using an oscilloscope, an electronic testing device that monitors electric impulses. An interpretation of the oscilloscope reading will determine which, if any, components need to be replaced. This type of routine diagnosis should be performed at intervals of 10,000 or 15,000 miles. The 10,000-mile tuneup — plugs, points, condenser — is now a thing of the past.

The distributor cap and rotor should be removed and the central portion of the distributor lubricated at regular intervals. This is the part of the distributor that houses the centrifugal advances of the unit; these are necessary for good fuel economy and drivability. If the advance

The central portion of the distributor should be lubricated at this spot at regular intervals, to maintain good fuel economy and driveability. In some cars, this is a complicated job and should only be attempted by a professional mechanic.

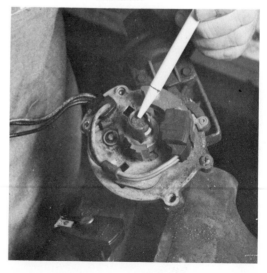

mechanism wears, or sticks because of lack of lubrication, mileage and performance will both suffer. On some cars, the advance mechanism is housed right underneath the rotor and can easily be reached for lubrication. On others, lubrication of the advance mechanism can only be accomplished by disassembling the distributor. This is a job for a professional mechanic and should not be attempted by a do-it-yourselfer.

Automobiles in which the electronic ignition module is installed in the distributor itself require specific service for that module. Every 30,000 to 50,000 miles, the distributor should be disassembled and the module removed from the distributor mounting pad. Once the module has been removed, a special heat-dissipating silicone lubricant should be spread between the module and the distributor mounting pad. The action of this lubricant will safeguard the module from being disabled by excessive heat, which is probably the most common electronic distributor problem.

On some cars, the module is mounted on the inside fender panel, or elsewhere within the engine compartment, rather than inside the distributor. This type of installation will involve external wiring. This wiring should periodically be broken at the connections, and the connections should be cleaned and preferably coated very lightly with the same heat-dissipating silicone lubricant mentioned above. The connections can then be reassembled and the wiring put back in place. This simple procedure can prevent corrosion, which cuts down resistance to the low-voltage currents traveling between the distributor and the module — resistance that can cause a car to stall or hesitate, especially as the engine first warms up.

On any car, electronic ignition or otherwise, the spark plug wires, distributor cap, and rotor should be inspected periodically and replaced as necessary. Remove the cap and look at the rotor tip to see if it is burned or shows signs of black oxidation. If so, the rotor should be replaced, *not* filed or cleaned with sandpaper. The terminals on the inside of the distributor cap should also be clean and free of oxidation. It, too, should be replaced when the telltale signs appear. Caps and rotor should be replaced together.

On the top of every distributor cap are a series of towers, one for each cylinder of the engine, where the spark plug wires connect. To check the contacts in the towers, pull the plug wires out *one at a time*, being careful not to damage them. If the metal surfaces of the contacts have any other than a bright, shiny appearance, the cap should be replaced — not cleaned. Dirty contacts in the cap can promote resistance between the cap and the spark plug wires, causing "crossfiring" between cylinders or making a cylinder skip because current is running to ground.

The spark plug wires themselves can be accurately checked only with an *ohmmeter*, a device for measuring electrical resistance in a conductor. The reading from the meter should be no more than 6,000 ohms for each; anything under 6,000 is acceptable, but if the reading exceeds the higher figure, it's time to replace the wires right away. If you don't have an

Testing Spark Plug Wires

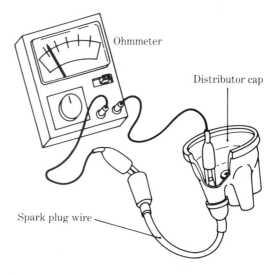

Ohmmeter

Distributor cap

Spark plug wire

ohmmeter, check the physical condition of the "boots" in which the plugs are seated and the insulating material that forms the outside of the wires. Cracking or deterioration means that it's time for replacement. Generally, spark plug wires have a useful life of from 20,000 to 40,000 miles or three to four years.

Spark Plugs

The one component of the ignition system that hasn't really changed over the years is the spark plug. The spark plug is a device that allows high-voltage electricity to enter the combustion chamber and then jump a gap with a spark that will ignite the air-fuel mixture. Spark plugs today are lasting longer than they used to, partly because of advances in plug technology, but primarily because of the absence

of lead in the gasoline we burn. Lead, which used to be used as an additive to boost gasoline octane, had a way of coating and fouling plug electrodes during combustion. After 10,000 or 15,000 miles of driving, a lead-burning plug's useful life was pretty much over. On today's cars, spark plugs last a lot longer — although how much longer depends on driving conditions. Many manufacturers are now claiming that plugs will last 30,000 miles. Under ideal circumstances, there is truth to this claim. But stop-and-go city driving, short trips during which the engine never really gets warm, and driving at high speeds all contribute to shortening spark plug life. Since one or another of these habits is shared by just about everyone

The Spark Plug

Ribs on the insulator increase its surface length, reducing the chance of a high voltage spark jumping to the ground.

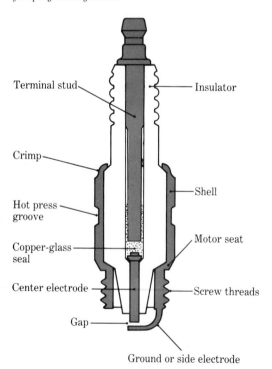

Terminal stud

Insulator

Crimp

Shell

Hot press groove

Copper-glass seal

Motor seat

Center electrode

Screw threads

Gap

Ground or side electrode

Spark Plug Heat Range

In a cold spark plug, heat developed during combustion has a short distance to travel from the electrode tip of the plug, through the insulator contact, the sealing gasket, the shell, and on into the cylinder head. In a hot plug, because the heat path is longer, the tip retains more heat and is able to burn off deposits caused by low-speed driving.

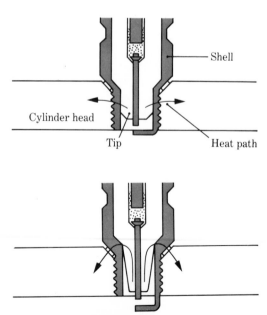

Shell

Cylinder head

Tip

Heat path

who gets behind a wheel, it's a good idea to replace the spark plugs every 12,000 miles.

As with the rest of the electronic ignition system, the best way to check the performance of spark plugs is with an oscilloscope. If an oscilloscope isn't handy, remove the plugs, and check their color. The color of the plugs will tell you how well they are firing. The working end of the plug — the electrodes — should be a sandy brown. They should not be worn or eroded away, and they should be parallel

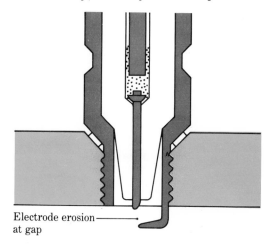

Electrode erosion at gap

to each other. If a spark plug needs to be cleaned, it can be sandblasted, the electrodes filed lightly, and then regapped. "Gapping" a spark plug means nothing more than setting the proper distance between the two electrodes. Your owner's manual will give the correct gap setting, which can be made by using a spark-gap tool — a series of dull metal blades calibrated to different thicknesses. After setting the gap, make sure the electrodes are parallel and that both are square-ended so that there is a large surface on both sides for the spark to jump from and to. If the plugs can be acceptably cleaned and regapped, they may be reinstalled. If not, or if there is irreversible damage, such as cracking of the ceramic body, they should be replaced regardless of how many miles remain according to the manufacturer's claims.

Other Electrical System Functions

The remainder of the electrical system in an automobile is given over primarily to powering lights, dashboard functions, and accessories. There are two ways to check on how the system is doing these jobs: visually, and with a voltmeter. The visual method needs no explanation: are the lights on? Does the radio play? The purpose of the voltmeter check is to determine if there is a voltage drop (loss of voltage) throughout the circuits. Such a drop might result in a dimming of headlights and taillights that might not otherwise be immediately apparent.

A voltmeter or a test light can be used to troubleshoot a malfunctioning circuit. Start at the fuse panel. Don't trust the outward appearance of a fuse. To be sure, run the contact of a test light from one end of a fuse to the other while the fuse is firmly in its socket. Turn on the circuit. That will establish whether or not there is electricity flowing through the fuse. If the fuse is sound, and, say, a headlight is out, go to the bulb end of the circuit. Take out the bulb, and insert the voltmeter or the test light. Then turn the circuit on — if you get a reading from the voltmeter, or if the test light goes on, you've probably got a bad bulb. That's simple enough to replace. If the voltmeter and/or the test light fail to function, the problem is farther up in the line. Take the voltmeter and backtrack along the circuit toward the switch and the power source, breaking the circuit at each connection and retesting until you find the "open" — that is, the point beyond which electricity is failing to pass. It may be at the switch, fuse panel, or power source. If the fuse is good, and there is no apparent voltage drop at any point in the wiring leading from the power source, there is a chance the test light or a new bulb still may not function. If that's the case, you have to use an ohmmeter to check the ground side of the circuit while the circuit is disconnected.

The Heart of the Matter: The Power System

The vast majority of today's automobiles are powered by one or the other of two main engine designs: diesel and gasoline. Both are *internal-combustion* engines, which operate on a heat-expansion principle. Fire is started in the combustion chambers, which causes the volatile gases trapped within to burn and expand and drive the pistons down. The downward motion of the pistons is picked up by a series of connecting rods and transferred to rotary motion by the crankshaft on which they are attached. This rotary

motion is fed out through the flywheel end of the engine to the other components of the drive train to make the car move along the road.

Although similar in many respects, the gasoline engine and the diesel engine have certain basic differences. In the gas engine, air and fuel are mixed externally, fed into the combustion chambers, and then ignited with the high-voltage spark with which we became familiar in the preceding chapter. In the diesel, only air is drawn into the engine through the intake system. The fuel is injected into each cyl-

The Internal Engine Components

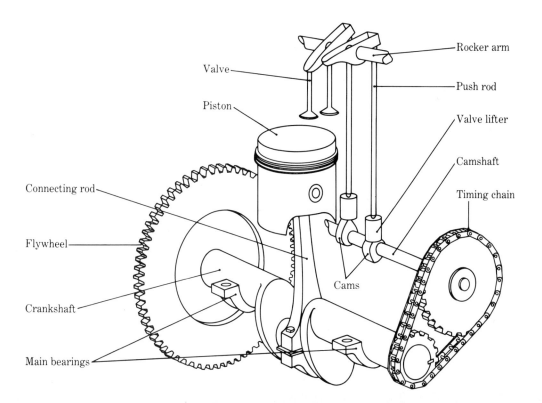

The Diesel Engine vs. the Gasoline Engine

The glow plug heats the pre-chamber to allow the diesel fuel to ignite. Without a glow plug, starting a diesel engine on a cold day is almost impossible.

Diesel Engine   Gasoline Engine

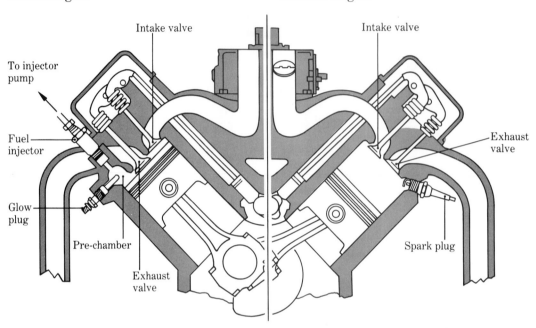

Intake valve

To injector pump

Fuel injector

Glow plug

Pre-chamber

Exhaust valve

Intake valve

Exhaust valve

Spark plug

How Diesel Engines Work

There was a time when the only diesel engines most of us encountered were in big trucks, stationary power plants, and the occasional Mercedes-Benz (in fact, 90 percent of the Mercedes cars sold in America are diesel-powered). Then came the gasoline shortages of the 1970s, and the fuel-efficient diesels became hot items.

How does a diesel differ from a gasoline engine? Perhaps we can best answer this question in terms of what the diesel doesn't have that the gas engine does — namely spark plugs, an ignition system, or a carburetor and fuel system of the type we've described in this chap-

ter. The diesel is a *compression ignition* engine. The compression ratio in a gasoline engine is usually 8 to 1, meaning that there is eight times the volume in each cylinder when the piston is at the bottom of its stroke than when it is at the top. In a diesel, this figure is *22 to 1*. The air in each cylinder is thus compressed much more tightly in the diesel, and that high compression translates into heat — at the top of the compression stroke, the air in a diesel combustion chamber is in the vicinity of 700°F.

Now let's look into the diesel's approach to fuel intake. Unlike the gas engine, the diesel does not have a throttle valve to limit the amount of fuel that enters the com-

bustion chamber. Instead, the valve in each cylinder of a diesel is open to atmospheric pressure at all times. On every intake stroke of the piston, the valve opens all the way and the chamber takes in as much air as it can accommodate.

As the piston nears the top of its compression stroke, the fuel injector, operated by the fuel-injection pump, injects a metered squirt of diesel fuel into the combustion chamber. The timing of this squirt is regulated by the turning of the engine, and its amount is determined by the position of the throttle — the farther down you push the gas pedal, the

inder only after this air has been tightly compressed, and it is the heat of this compressed air — there is no spark plug or other ignition device — that causes the fuel to burn.

The more popular by far of these two engine types is the gasoline engine, which accounts for more than 80 percent of the passenger cars on the road today. The diesel operates just less than 20 percent, with a tiny percentage powered by electricity or propane, the latter of which is burned in slightly modified gasoline engines. The gas engine is our concern in this book.

Getting Fuel to the Engine

In order to function correctly, the gasoline engine depends heavily on the electrical starting and ignition systems, which we learned about in the preceding chapter, and also on the *external fuel system*. This system is comprised of the fuel tank, fuel lines, fuel pump, carburetor or fuel-injection system, intake manifold, and the intake valves in the engine. Gasoline is drawn from the fuel tank, through the lines, through the fuel pump, and into the

more diesel fuel goes into the chambers and the faster you go.

When the diesel fuel meets the compressed, superheated air above the piston, it catches fire. The rest is the same as in a gas engine: the hot, expanding combustion gases drive the piston down and the exhaust stroke follows. The diesel engine, then, differs from the gasoline engine only in the type of fuel it burns, and the way that fuel is ignited. The diesel block, of course, is also built heavier than a gas engine block, to accommodate the pressures associated with that higher compression ratio.

engine compartment. On a carburetor-equipped engine, the fuel is next fed into a float bowl in the carburetor. The float bowl is a device that stores enough fuel to meet any of the driver's demands: acceleration, full power driving uphill, towing a trailer, or any other load demand.

The fuel in the carburetor is mixed with air and forced into the combustion chambers, primarily because of the difference between the atmospheric pressure outside the engine and the vacuum created on the inside by the ongoing processes of combustion and piston motion. The air-fuel mixture is forced into the intake manifold through the various passageways (remember, we aren't talking about fuel injection, which operates differently).

The volume of the fuel mixture admitted in this process directly affects the speed of the car. The acceleration of a gasoline engine is completely controlled by the throttle position, and by the throttle-plate position in the carburetor. By opening the throttle farther we admit more air; by admitting more air we draw more fuel into the cylinders and the car goes faster. The more fuel and air there are in the cylinders, the hotter the fires that burn there. That increase in heat intensity drives the pistons down faster and gives them more energy with which to turn the crankshaft.

The carburetor has seven basic circuits: the float, idle, and choke circuits; and the low-speed, high-speed, power, and accelerator-pump circuits. The *float* circuit is responsible for keeping enough fuel in the carburetor to meet the driver's demands. The *idle* circuit runs the car while the engine is idling, which can be up to 1,200 or 1,300 rpm (revolutions of the crankshaft per minute). *Idling* doesn't mean that the car has to be standing still; on a four-cylinder engine, 1,200 to 1,300 rpm can bring the car up to around 30 mph, and on some of the late-model V-8 engines, it could be translated into a road speed of 50 or 55.

The *choke* circuit simply makes sure that there is enough gasoline going into the engine during a cold start to get it to fire and run. (The reason cold starts can be difficult is that low temperatures make it hard to get enough fuel into the combustion chamber to vaporize and ignite.)

The *low-speed* circuit is a combination of the idle circuit and a special low-speed passage in the carburetor. It controls fuel flow while the engine is operating above idle but still not very fast — up to about 2,500 rpm. Since the idle circuit is part of low-speed operation, a misadjustment of the idle can seriously affect

a car's performance at lower speeds.

The *high-speed* circuit controls fuel flow while the car is cruising at highway speeds. It is a lean circuit, designed for fuel efficiency (by *lean* we mean that there is a smaller amount of fuel in relation to the volume of air introduced into the combustion chambers). However, even at higher speeds it is sometimes necessary to extract more power from the engine in order to climb hills or tow a heavy load. This is the job of the *power* circuit, which is usually controlled by a combination of accelerator-pedal position and the intake-manifold vacuum in the engine. This vacuum level is a good indication of the severity of the load under which the engine is operating. Low vacuum means high load; that's when you're pressing

The Mechanical Pump Fuel System

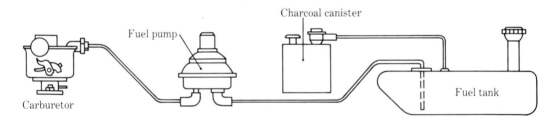

The Electronic Fuel-Injection System

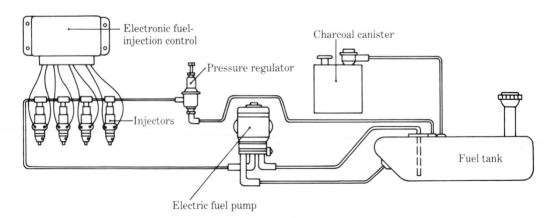

The Carburetor

Float Circuit

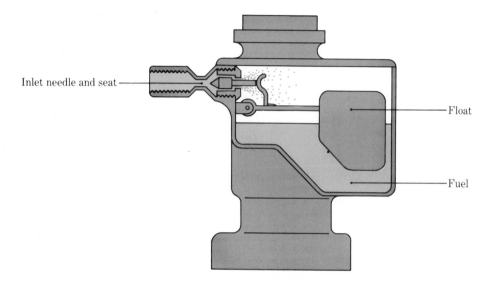

Inlet needle and seat —

— Float

— Fuel

Idle Circuit

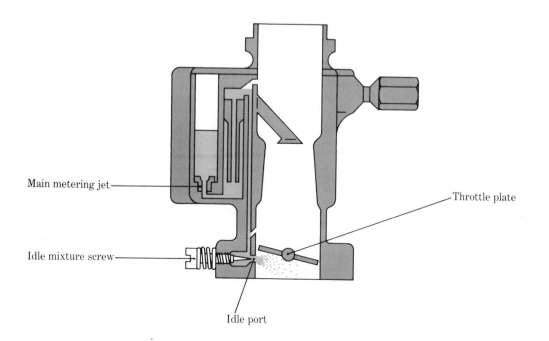

Main metering jet —

— Throttle plate

Idle mixture screw —

Idle port

The Carburetor (cont.)

High-Speed Circuit

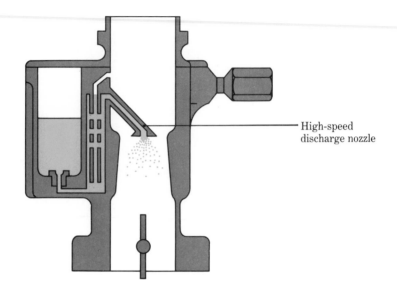

High-speed
discharge nozzle

Accelerator-Pump Circuit

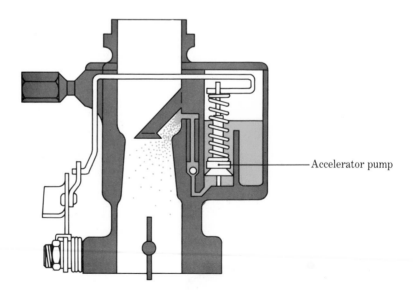

Accelerator pump

down on the gas pedal and trying to go faster. High vacuum means low load, with the engine running easily and capable of performing well on a lean fuel mixture. The power circuit simply changes the mixture in response to changes in engine load.

The *accelerator-pump* circuit of the carburetor assures instantaneous response when the driver presses quickly on the accelerator — for instance, on a freeway entrance ramp or when passing another vehicle. It does this simply by injecting a sharp spurt of gasoline through the throat of the carburetor into the intake manifold so that the driver's response to the situation, translated through the throttle, results in the necessary increase of engine power.

The Four-Stroke Cycle

Once the fuel has entered the engine through the intake manifold, it goes into the combustion chambers through the intake valves. In a four-stroke-cycle engine — the kind of engine that predominates among gasoline-powered passenger cars — there are two valves in each cylinder head: an intake valve and an exhaust valve. The valves are controlled by a *camshaft*. As we'll see later, the camshaft turns at a precise rate governed by the rotation of the crankshaft, to which it is geared.

The four strokes of a four-stroke-cycle engine are the intake, compression, power, and exhaust strokes. During the *intake* stroke, the intake valve is open and the piston is moving downward in the cylinder. As it moves, the volume of the combustion chamber (the area in the cylinder above the head of the piston) gets larger. That sudden expansion is what creates the above-mentioned vacuum that draws the air-fuel mixture in. If the throttle is open and the carburetor is working correctly, atmospheric pressure on the outside of the engine (and the fuel along with it) will rush to fill the vacuum.

Once the piston gets to the bottom of the cylinder and the bottom of its stroke, the intake valve closes and the *compression stroke* begins. The crankshaft continues to turn and begins to push the piston back up in the cylinder. Since both valves are now closed and the spark plug is screwed tightly into the only other outlet of the cylinder, the air-fuel vapor above the piston has nowhere to go. It is thus compressed, to a ratio of eight to one. This ratio simply means that when the piston is at the lowest point in its stroke cycle, or "bottom dead center," the volume of the combustion chamber above is eight times what it is when the piston is at the top point in the cycle. (Eight to one is the average compression ratio in today's automobiles. Higher compression ratios have been used in the past, but they require leaded gasoline with a higher octane rating. Octane is a measure of the fuel's volatility.)

With the piston at the top of its cycle and the combustion chamber at its smallest, the air-fuel mixture is very tightly compressed. Compression accentuates the explosive force of a volatile material. If you sprinkle gunpowder or the chemical components of dynamite on the ground, the material would simply burn. But pack such stuff tightly, in a cartridge in a rifle chamber or in a stiff cardboard tube, and the outcome changes dramatically. So it is with the air-fuel mixture in an engine's combustion chamber. When the ignition system sends a spark arcing across the gap of the spark plug, the tightly compressed mixture is set on fire. As the burning gases expand, they thrust the piston downward in the cylinder according to the same principle that sends a bullet from a gun. But the piston isn't going far; only to the bottom of the cylinder, where its connecting rod turns the crankshaft. This is called the *power stroke*.

At the end of the power stroke, with the piston again at bottom dead center, the exhaust valve at the top of the chamber opens and the piston again begins

The Four-Stroke Cycle

Intake

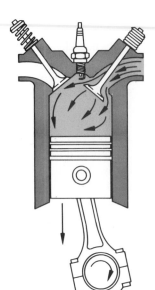

Compression

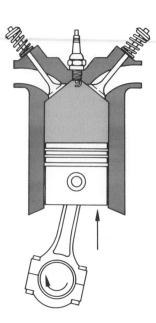

Power

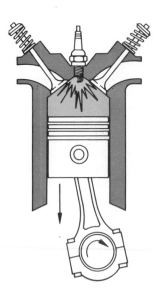

Exhaust

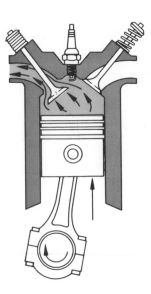

moving upward. The gases remaining after combustion exit the chamber through the exhaust valve and move into the exhaust manifold and through the front pipe, catalytic converter, muffler, and tailpipe and then out of the car. This, then, is the *exhaust stroke*, the fourth and final stroke of the four-stroke cycle.

The Valve Train

The parts that make this sequence of events possible may be broken down into several different subsystems. One is the *valve train*, which consists of the timing gears, timing chain or belt, camshaft, push rods, and the hydraulic valve lifters or tappets.

The camshaft turns at one-half the speed of the crankshaft — two turns of the crankshaft equal one turn of the camshaft. This ratio is necessary because it takes two turns of the crankshaft to complete the entire four-stroke cycle, each stroke occupying 180 degrees of the crankshaft's rotation but only 90 degrees of the rotation of the camshaft, which operates the valves. The precision of the speed differential between the two shafts is maintained by the cogged belt, or more usually chain, that connects them. (The exception would be engines in which two gears mesh, for a direct-gear drive between crankshaft and camshaft.)

The motion of the spinning camshaft is transferred from the eccentrically shaped cams to the valves via the *push rods*, which extend up through the engine block and cylinder head in conventional engine designs having the camshaft at the bottom and the valves at the top of the cylinders. At the valves themselves, we find either *hydraulic valve lifters* or *tappets*, depending upon the design of the engine. The hydraulic valve lifters are devices that automatically take up any play or slack in the system, keep its operation quiet, and prevent the valves from

hanging open and burning. Tappets are adjustable valves set to a particular clearance between the camshaft and the lifter so that noise will be at a minimum while the valve still has room for heat expansion and contraction.

At the point where it emerges from the top of the cylinder head, each push rod makes contact with a *rocker arm*, a see-saw-like device mounted on a stationary shaft or ball stud. As the push rod pushes one end of the rocker arm up, the other end is pushed down onto the valve stem, opening the valve against the pressure of the valve spring. Depending on which valve is being operated, this either allows the air-fuel mixture to get into the cylinder or the exhaust gases to get out. Once the push rod rides over the high point on the cam beneath it, it begins to fall, allowing the valve to close through the action of the valve springs. The spring tension brings the valve down tightly into its seat. The valve is thus opened by the cam, but closed by the spring.

An alternative to the standard push rod–rocker arm setup we've described here is the *overhead cam* engine design. This involves eliminating the push rods by simply mounting the camshaft above the valves, on top of the cylinder head. With no push rods or rocker arms, we manage to avoid a lot of excess motion and can usually make the engine more powerful. The camshaft in an overhead-cam engine is driven by a cogged timing belt or timing chain. This belt, or chain, must be changed periodically — some manufacturers recommend 40,000-mile intervals, some 60,000 miles. If the belt strips or stretches out of shape, the valves and pistons could come into contact with each other and the engine could be seriously damaged.

Valve seats and valve faces are precision-ground, so that when they close, they will hold compression and combustion tightly within the cylinder. When they leak, performance will suffer, making it necessary to perform a valve job on the engine.

Another potential problem is burning oil (engine lubricating oil introduced from outside the cylinders) because valve stem/valve guide clearances get too large, or valve seals are worn. The valve stem runs up and down inside a valve guide in the cylinder head; the clearance between stem and valve is usually about one one-thousandth of an inch. If it gets much larger, valve action will get sloppy and oil will find its way into the combustion chamber. In addition to the telltale exhaust color (see chapter 8), rough running of the engine at low speeds is a sign of oil burning caused by bad valve seating.

Essentially, though, modern advances in design, technology, machin-ing, and materials have reduced valve service requirements to a minimum. Gone are the days of valve grinding at 30,000 miles and complete valve jobs at 60,000. Today, it's entirely possible to run an engine for 100,000 to 200,000 miles without ever touching the valves — *provided* the engine is kept in good tune and the oil is changed at recommended intervals to keep the hydraulic lifters, camshaft, and valve guides in top condition. When valve-system servicing is necessary, however, it's important that it be done promptly and professionally.

The Timing Belt and Overhead Cam

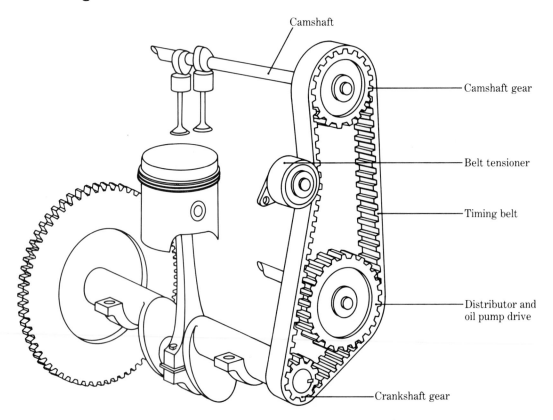

Camshaft

Camshaft gear

Belt tensioner

Timing belt

Distributor and oil pump drive

Crankshaft gear

The Pistons, the Crankshaft, and the Oiling System

The pistons, moving up and down in their cylinders, comprise the next important part of the internal-combustion engine. There are two important things about pistons that might seem to contradict what the layman assumes to be true. First, pistons are not perfectly round, and second, they do not make full direct contact with the cylinder walls. Pistons are actually slightly oval in shape to allow for heat expansion during operation: when the engine is cold, two sides guide the piston along the cylinder walls, with the other sides filling out as temperatures increase. If this were not the case, the pistons would have to be made too small and would "slap" in their cylinders when cold.

As for contact with the walls, this is actually made by the *piston rings*. The piston itself sits back one- or two-thousandths of an inch from the cylinder wall; any greater tolerance and oil consumption would increase and the engine would run noisily. The rings are thin circles of tempered spring steel that fit into parallel grooves along the circumference of the piston and maintain the pressure against the cylinder walls. Most pistons have three rings each. The top two are *compression* rings, which keep combustion and compression in the cylinder above the piston. The bottom ring is the *oil* ring, which scrapes the oil off the cylinder walls and returns it to the crankcase so the engine does not burn excessive amounts of oil. The oil ring does leave a thin film of oil on the cylinder walls to lubricate the two compression rings, though, so they do not wear out the engine.

Engine oil is more than just a lubricant. During the power and exhaust strokes of the piston, it acts as a seal between the rings and the cylinder walls, which prevents the escape of combustion by-products into the crankcase. And during the compression stroke, this same sealing effect ensures that sufficient pressure is maintained in the combustion chamber. In fact, the contact of rings and cylinder walls alone would not be enough to provide compression if the oil were not present.

When piston rings wear out or lose their temper, the result is increased oil consumption and the condition known as "blowby." In blowby, the by-products of combustion find their way into the crankcase below the pistons, increase temperature and pressure in the crankcase, and cause the engine to smoke out of the crankcase breathers. On cars equipped with positive crankcase ventilation — now a part of most emissions systems — blowby can even be responsible for driving oil up into the air cleaner.

Each piston also has a hole running perpendicular to its sides, called the *wrist pin hole*. Here is located the wrist pin, by which the piston is attached to its *connecting rod*. The connecting rod joins the piston to the crankshaft. The wrist pin allows the rod to move back and forth with the motion of the connecting rod bearing on the crankshaft as the piston travels up and down.

The points of contact between the connecting-rod bearings and the crankshaft are yet another spot in which an extremely small clearance — about one- or two-thousandths of an inch — is essential. These bearings are kept lubricated by oil pressure provided by the oil pump. Pressure feeds the oil up through holes drilled in the crankshaft to serve each bearing. If pressure is lost to any individual bearing, the bearing is ruined, and very likely the engine is ruined along with it.

Oil pressure and volume are important to other parts of the engine as well. The cylinder walls are kept lubricated by throwoff from the bearings; if a bearing is fitted properly, there will be just the right amount of oil on the walls to lubricate the pistons and rings. When the bearings wear, they can allow too much oil to get up onto the cylinder walls. The result will be the familiar situation in which the engine is said to "burn oil." Using an oil that is too thin for the engine's requirements can also make this happen. Thin oil will run past the bearings too rapidly, causing oil consumption in the cylinders and overall poor engine lubrication. The important thing to remember here is that the quality and specifications of engine oil are just as important as keeping it clean and free of contaminants.

The crankshaft is held to the engine block and allowed to rotate by *main bearings*, which also serve as the main galleys through which the oil comes to the crankshaft. The flow of oil from the oil pump is split at the entrance to the engine block, with some going to the camshaft and valve train and the rest to each of the main bearings. If everything is working properly, this oil is distributed through the main bearings and the drill holes in the crankshaft to lubricate the connecting rod journals. All this depends on the shape the main bearings are in. If a bearing is too loose (again, one- to two-thousandths of an inch is the norm for tolerances), the oil will leak down into the pan at that point and will go no farther in the engine. The engine will then fail through lack of lubrication.

The front main bearing has a small drip hole through which oil flows to lubricate the timing gears and timing chain. On a car having an overhead camshaft driven by a timing belt, no such lubrication is necessary.

As was indicated above, the oil in an automobile engine does not just slosh around aimlessly; it is pumped at pressure

Engine Oil: What Those Letters and Numbers Mean

Oil performs a three-way task of lubricating, sealing, and cooling within an engine. It should come as no surprise, then, that the type and quality of the oil we use have a tremendous effect on engine performance and longevity. Engine oil should always be of at least the minimum quality acceptable under the terms of the owner's manual, and should have the additives necessary to prevent foaming and stand up to high temperatures and pressures. If you pay attention to the way oil is rated and labeled, you'll have no problem meeting manual specifications.

All motor oils are rated by the American Petroleum Institute, and those ratings are coded on oil cans according to an "S" series: SA, SB, SC, SD, SE, and SF. The *S* indicates that the oil is acceptable for gasoline engines, and the remaining letter indicates conformance to certain minimum specification levels. Since the late seventies, most cars have been using only the highest-grade oils: SE and SF. They are designed to withstand high pressures and high operating temperatures, especially in small four-cylinder engines.

Diesel engine oils are rated according to a similar scheme, but the first letter is *C*, for *commercial*. For diesels, CC and CD are the highest-rated oils. Sometimes, the printing of both the "S" and "C" ratings on a can of oil — for instance, SE/CD — can lead a buyer into mistakenly thinking that all SE oils are acceptable in cars requiring CD, and vice versa. This is not true. Buy *only* the oil specified in your owner's manual, and don't make assumptions based on cross-referencing in other manuals.

The other system of oil rating is numerical, and it refers to the oil's viscosity. Viscosity is a measure of a liquid's ability to flow. Most automotive oils sold today are in the 10 to 20 viscosity range. (The "SAE" next to the viscosity number stands for Society of Automotive Engineers, the parent testing agency.) The right oil viscosity depends on the temperatures likely to be experienced during driving. For below-zero temperatures, a 10 will usually be acceptable, while a 30 or 40 is required for distance driving on hot summer days. Often, oil is blended so that the performance characteristics of each viscosity level will come into play as necessary. The letter *W* in a blend rating stands for *winter* and indicates that the oil was tested under winter conditions and will not congeal as fast as heavier summer oils when the temperature is below zero.

in a continuous cycle. The first thing the oil encounters on leaving the crankcase is a filter screen, located at the oil pump or intake oil galley. This screen, which sits about an inch above the bottom of the crankcase, filters out the larger contaminant particles in the engine. The reason for that inch of clearance from the bottom is to provide room for sediment to build up in the crankcase without being drawn up into the engine, where it could do serious harm through abrasion.

The next stop along the oil-flow path is the *oil pump*. This is a positive-displacement device, meaning that all of the oil drawn into it is pushed out at a higher pressure than that at which it entered. It is driven mechanically, from either the crankshaft or the camshaft of the engine. On the outlet side of the pump

The Engine Oiling System

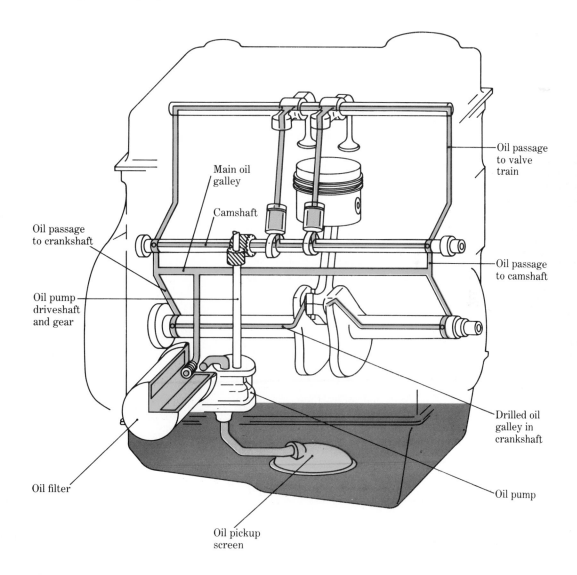

Oil passage to valve train

Main oil galley

Camshaft

Oil passage to crankshaft

Oil passage to camshaft

Oil pump driveshaft and gear

Drilled oil galley in crankshaft

Oil filter

Oil pump

Oil pickup screen

is an *oil pressure relief valve*. This is a small but extremely important component that regulates the ambient oil pressure in the engine. Since the turning of the oil pump is directly related to the rotation of the engine, it's obvious that its output pressure will increase proportionately with engine speed. If this situation were left uncorrected, there would be too little pressure at low speeds and too much when the engine was running fast. At idle and at low speeds — especially low speeds under heavy loads, such as acceleration from a standing start — the spring-loaded valve adjusts to compensate for the slower movement of the pump. When the engine is running faster, or when the oil is cold or of too heavy a viscosity, the valve closes down and vents excess pressure back into the crankcase so that seals and other engine parts are not put under undue stress. The valve is pre-set at the recommended maximum oil presure for the car.

After passing through the pressure relief valve, the oil next goes into the removable *oil filter*, which on all modern engines is of the *full-flow* type: every drop of engine oil circulates through the filter on each pumping cycle. Some filters are single stage, some double stage, but all are completely modular in that the entire unit can be screwed off, discarded, and replaced (some older cars had a permanent filter housing, and only the inner element was replaced).

Inside each oil filter is a pressure-differential relief valve. If for any reason the filter should become plugged, this valve will automatically open and allow the oil to bypass the filter completely. The theory behind this feature is that a flow of dirty oil into the engine is better than no flow at all. That may be true — but clean oil is better by far. Since a driver has absolutely no way of knowing if that differential relief valve has closed, and since contaminated oil will inevitably wear an engine down, an ironclad case can be made

for frequent, regular changes of both the oil *and the filter*. This is especially true for cars driven under "severe service" driving conditions: stop-and-go driving; repeated trips of less than 10 miles; heavy traveling on dusty roads; and driving for 60 days or more during winter when temperatures are below freezing. All of these conditions can cause filters to plug up prematurely. Despite manufacturers' recommendations for oil and filter change intervals of 10,000 miles or more, a more realistic schedule would involve changes as frequently as every 5,000 or even 3,000 miles, depending upon driving conditions. This is the cheapest and one of the most important maintenance operations that can be performed on an engine.

We've seen that oil has an important part to play as both a sealant and a lubricant. But engine oil is also a *coolant;* it carries heat away from the undersides of the pistons and the cylinder walls, as well as other parts inaccessible to the cooling system. This heat is then dissipated through the crankshaft. This is why it isn't good to run a car with the engine oil "down a quart." The less oil there is, the hotter the remaining oil gets, and the sooner it begins to break down and oxidize. Once oil begins to oxidize, its lubricating and sealing value diminishes and engine parts become prone to wear.

The Cooling System

All internal-combustion engines develop a tremendous amount of heat, which can damage vital parts if it is not safely dissipated. Aside from the above-mentioned cooling function performed by oil circulation, there are two ways to get rid of excess heat: air cooling and water cooling. Most of today's engines are water-cooled, although their operation actually involves some combination of the two principles.

A water-cooling system comprises a radiator, water pump, hoses, thermostat, fan belt, and radiator fan, along with the cooling jackets built into the cylinder block and head castings through which the coolant flows. The circulating coolant picks up heat from the various engine parts. The heated coolant then flows into the *radiator*. If the coolant travels through the radiator slowly enough, and if there is enough air flowing over and around the radiator, the engine heat carried in the coolant will be dissipated in the atmo-sphere and the cycle of cooling can continue. The coolant exits the radiator through the bottom radiator hose and heads back to the water pump and into the engine to pick up more heat.

We remarked earlier that a water-cooled engine is really partly cooled by

The Cooling System

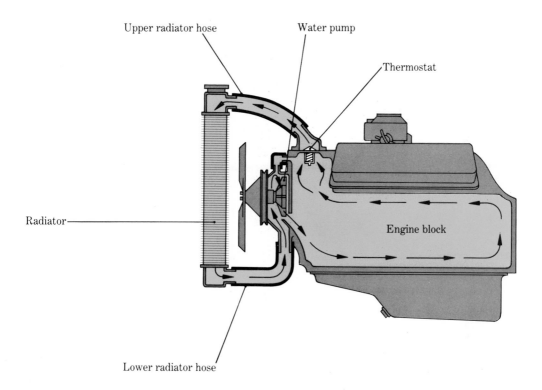

Upper radiator hose
Water pump
Thermostat
Radiator
Engine block
Lower radiator hose

The Air-Cooled Engine

Nowadays, the water-cooled automobile engine reigns supreme. But air-cooled engine designs have been used in quite a few different cars, including the old Chevrolet Corvair and the legendary Volks-wagen bug. As you might expect, in an air-cooled engine it is air, rather than a liquid coolant, that dissipates the excess heat built up during operation. The air is driven over the engine, in what is known as a "ram air" effect, by a strategi-cally placed fan. (On a motorcycle, the simple action of moving along the road takes the place of the fan, which is why it isn't good to leave your bike standing with the motor running for very long.)

As long as there is sufficient engine surface, enough air, and a smoothly functioning fan, the air-cooling principle works quite well. But if any of the air passages become clogged, or if the fan stops working — for instance, if the belt breaks — the engine will overheat.

air. This is because of the action of the *fan*, belt-driven off the engine, which forces air through the radiator and helps the circulating coolant dissipate its collected heat. In the preceding chapter, we saw how a loose fan belt could adversely affect the alternator's electrical output. It can also keep the fan from turning at the optimum speed, thus contributing to engine overheating.

It would be nice if a simple process of circulating water could take care of all of an engine's cooling requirements. But today's engines run very hot — hotter than the boiling point of water. The coolant cannot be allowed to boil, because if air bubbles form, its flow will be blocked and the entire system will be rendered ineffective. There are two ways of keeping this from happening, and both find their place in modern cars. One is to mix the water to a fifty-fifty ratio with propylene glycol, commonly known as antifreeze and at one time primarily used in the winter.

But antifreeze is anti*boil* as well: the half-and-half mixture prescribed here has a boiling point of 240°F, rather than water's 212°F.

The second measure taken to keep the coolant from boiling is to apply pressure to the system. Every increase of one pound per square inch (p.s.i.) of pressure will increase the boiling point of coolant in a closed system by 3°F. The radiator pressure caps used on most cars today exert a pressure of 15 to 17 p.s.i., for an additional margin of 45° to 51°F before a boiling point is reached. If that pressure is exceeded, of course, the cap will automatically vent.

The *thermostat* is an important part of the cooling system. It's basically a temperature-regulated valve that controls the rate at which coolant flows between the engine and the radiator, and consequently influences the operating temperature of the engine. The thing to remember about the thermostat is that it has to keep the engine temperature *above* a certain level, as well as below another. Today's engines are designed to run most efficiently at

Keep It Cool

Have you ever been stuck in traffic on the hottest day of the year? As you poke along at a snail's pace, you notice all of the cars pulled over to the side of the road with their hoods up and clouds of steam coming from the engine compartments.

It slowly dawns on you that you and your car could soon wind up in the same situation. Your palms are now sweaty, but not from the heat, and you wonder what measures you might take to avoid the party at the side of the road.

First, turn off the air conditioner and open the windows. If the car is equipped with automatic transmission, shift into neutral at each stop and slightly accelerate the engine. This will cause the fan on most cars to run faster, drawing more air into the radiator. It will also cause the water pump to run faster, circulating the water through the cooling system more quickly. Be sure to let the engine return to idle before putting the automatic transmission back into gear.

If the engine temperature gauge shows that the car is getting close to the danger zone, or if the red temperature light comes on, here is a trick that might get you through: turn the heater on full blast at the highest heat setting. Running the heater — which is actually an auxiliary radiator — will cool the engine down a bit. You may suffer for a while from the extra heat, but it'll be better than being hot under the collar by the side of the road.

temperatures approaching 200°F. If a modern engine doesn't run hot enough, fuel will be wasted through incomplete vaporization in the combustion chambers, and the exhaust will be excessively laden with hydrocarbons and carbon monoxide. Also, it's quite possible that spark advance mechanisms and components of the computer system will not turn on when they are supposed to if the engine is running too cool. Thus it is essential that a thermostat be replaced only with another unit of the type installed by the manufacturer. Taking out the factory-specified thermostat and replacing it with a cooler-operating model — what used to be called a summer thermostat — is a recipe for trouble.

Cooling-system maintenance is not complicated. Once a year, or whenever else you happen to be looking under the hood, check the hoses, hose clamps, and belts. Check the coolant level periodically and replenish with the right mix of antifreeze and water as necessary. Every other year, you may want to flush the old coolant from the car and replace it with a new solution.

Engine Configurations

The terms by which engines are known — V-8, straight-six, V-6, etc. — are all basically shorthand for the ways in which the cylinders are arranged. Back before the V-8 assumed virtually standard status among American engines in the mid-1950s, the most common engines were the *in-line* or *straight* designs. This meant that there

Engine Configurations

Opposed or pancake 4 cylinder

V-6 cylinder

In-line 4 cylinder

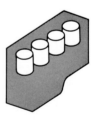

Opposed or pancake 6 cylinder

V-8 cylinder

In-line 6 cylinder

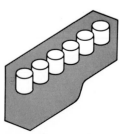

were four, six, or eight cylinders lined up in a row, all sharing a common crankshaft. The valves in this type of engine were either mounted beside the pistons in what was called an "L-head," "side-pocket," or "flathead" design. Or, the valves were placed above the pistons in the cylinder head for an overhead valve or "valve-in-head" design. The latter involves the push-rod and rocker-arm assembly with which we became familiar earlier, except in overhead-cam designs, which eliminate these extra components.

As automobile technology advanced, engineers began to grow dissatisfied with the in-line design. One superficial reason was sheer length, especially for eight-cylinder engines. This may have given thirties cars their classic appearance, but it was a bit unwieldy. A more important reason was crankshaft vibration. The longer a crankshaft is, the more torsional twisting is involved in its rotary motion — hence vibration and a less-than-smooth ride. There were also problems with fuel distribution, since the front and rear cylinders in an in-line arrangement are so far from the central carburetor. During its long trip through the intake manifold from the middle to the ends of such an engine, some of the fuel in the air-fuel mixture would actually come out of suspension. While the plugs in the middle cylinders would be fouling, plugs at the ends would be burning out from lean, overheated conditions. Why? It's simple: the farther the fuel mixture has to travel, the more fuel drops out of suspension. The end cylinders will get more air than gasoline. As the amount of liquid in the fuel diminishes, heat buildup in the affected cylinders increases, due to the absence of the humidity that would otherwise carry heat away from the valves and plugs. So, the end plugs would burn out prematurely.

The answer to the engineers' dilemma was the v-type engine, which was achieved by cutting a straight-eight in half, tilting the two halves toward each other at the bottom, and connecting the eight pistons to a common crankshaft at an angle. (The original V-8s were flat-

Fuel Injection

It wasn't so long ago that we encountered fuel injection only in race cars and exotic European imports. But now, fuel injection for the masses is available on foreign and domestic automobiles alike.

Although it remains a mystery to many, fuel injection is nothing more than its names implies: it is a precise method of injecting fuel into the intake air stream, rather than allowing it to be drawn in through a conventional carburetor by the combination of engine vacuum and atmospheric pressure. The fuel is carefully metered and sprayed into the intake under pressure, so that waste is kept to a minimum and both performance and economy benefit.

There are three basic types of fuel-injection systems. The first two, which come under the heading of *ported* injection, inject fuel directly into the manifold near the intake valve of each cylinder. These are the *constant* (or mechanical) and *electronic* systems. In the mechanical version, a fuel distributor mounted on the engine regularly meters fuel to the injection nozzles. The newer electronic system depends upon a microcomputer to read all of the engine's ongoing functions and send a signal to the injectors, which pulse fuel on command into the intake system.

The remaining approach to fuel injection is called the *throttle-body* or *single-point* system. This is what you'll find on most domestic fuel-injected cars. Instead of using a fuel injector for each cylinder, the single-point version relies on only one or two injectors, mounted in the intake manifold in place of the carburetor.

Any of these three fuel-injection options will offer more precise metering of fuel than is afforded by carburetion and will usually reduce emissions as well as squeeze more power and mileage out of each gallon of gasoline. Given today's increasingly stringent pollution and mpg regulations, fuel injection has become an important facet of contemporary automobile engineering.

heads; the overhead valve design came later.) These engines ran smoother because there was far less torsional twisting in the shorter, stiffer crankshafts. Nor did the fuel have as far to go, which solved the distribution problems that had plagued the in-lines.

Concerns over fuel economy have ended the heyday of the big V-8s, but there are still plenty of smaller and mid-size ones being made. Along with the V-6, V-4, and straight-four, and to some extent the straight-six, they provide the power for today's automobile fleet.

Dinosaur

During the Prohibition years of the late twenties and early thirties, people looked to the automobile for an extra kick. For those who could afford it, one of the biggest kicks of all was available from multi-cylinder behemoths like the V-12 Lincoln Zephyr, the Packard Twin-Six, and the grand boat pictured above: the Cadillac V-16.

Two words describe the sixteen-cylinder Caddy: smooth and powerful. Packing two banks of eight cylinders each into this monster also meant that you could

barely see the radiator from the driver's seat, which fit right in with the long-hood mystique of the era — a far cry from the profile associated with the efficient little transverse fours of today.

The weight, size, and cost of the big twelves and sixteens eventually proved their undoing. But as the Jazz Age passed into the long eclipse of the Great Depression, they put a lot of car at the command of a privileged few.

M.D.C.

Power to the Wheels: The Drive Train

The drive train of an automobile is a series of gears, shafts, clutches, and hydraulic devices, all of which serve two basic purposes: to transfer power from the engine to the drive wheels; and to change the ratio of the gears through which that power is delivered, so there is always an optimum amount of torque relative to engine speed. This second function is necessary because of an unavoidable characteristic of the internal-combustion engine — its power increases in proportion to its speed, so that at very low speeds there is very little power. If the engine were con- nected directly to the rear wheels with no transmission, you wouldn't be able to start the car and roll off smoothly.

Also, there are times when we need to have the engine disconnected from the drive wheels, such as when the engine is warming up, when the car is idling in traffic, or when repairs or adjustments require the engine to be running. This capability is afforded by a "neutral" position in the transmission, and, in standard transmissions, by a clutch.

This disconnection of engine from transmission must also be effected when

The Manual Clutch

- Clutch cable
- Pedal return spring
- Pedal pivot point
- Clutch pedal
- Throwout bearing
- Bell housing
- Clutch release lever
- Flywheel (bolted to crankshaft or engine)
- Clutch disc
- Clutch cover or pressure plate

How the Manual Clutch Works

Clutch Engaged

Engine turns and power is sent to the transmission input shaft

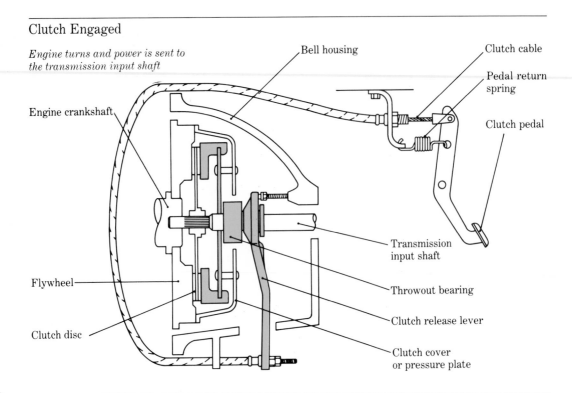

Bell housing

Clutch cable

Pedal return spring

Engine crankshaft

Clutch pedal

Transmission input shaft

Flywheel

Throwout bearing

Clutch release lever

Clutch disc

Clutch cover or pressure plate

Clutch Released

No drive connection between flywheel and transmission input shaft

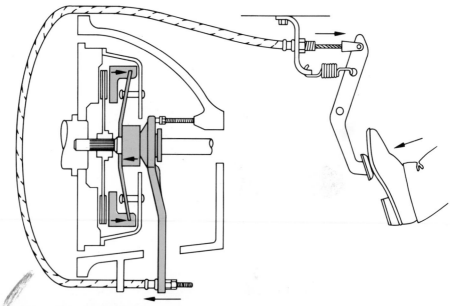

we wish to change from one gear to another. The gears must be allowed to mesh without power being applied, or else they will clash and grind. Disengaging the clutch allows one part of the transmission to freewheel, so that the gears will slide together smoothly.

The Manual Clutch

When you depress the clutch pedal in a car with standard transmission, you *disengage* the clutch and unhook the engine from the drive train. In some cars, there is a sophisticated mechanical linkage between the pedal and the clutch fork; in others, a hydraulically operated linkage. Still others employ a cable. Whichever method is used, the result is the same: the clutch fork connects with the throwout bearing to disengage the clutch.

What happens inside the clutch is best explained by looking at the procedure of lifting your foot off the pedal and *engaging* the clutch. This causes the *clutch disc* to be pressed firmly between the *flywheel* of the engine and an outer cover called the *pressure plate* through the action of the pressure plate's high-tension springs. The tight physical sandwiching of these three surfaces is what transmits the engine's power to the drive train. If the pedal is released slowly, the car goes off smoothly. When the clutch pedal is depressed (clutch disengaged), tension is removed from the springs and the pressure plate is pulled away from the clutch disc to unharness the engine.

Why an Automatic Needs No Clutch

As strange as it may seem, cars with automatic transmission have no mechanical connection between the engine and the drive train. (There is an exception in the higher gears on newer cars, which we'll look at a little later.) Instead, there is a *hydraulic torque converter*, or *fluid coupling*. The torque converter consists of a

The Torque Converter

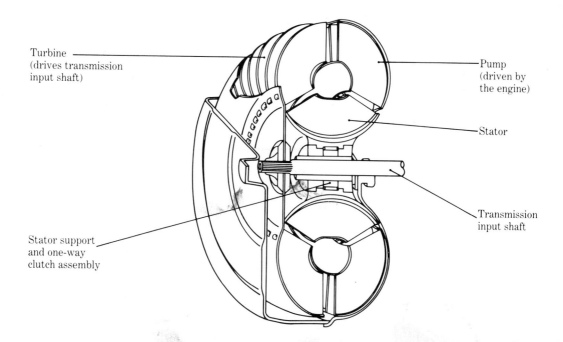

Turbine (drives transmission input shaft)

Pump (driven by the engine)

Stator

Stator support and one-way clutch assembly

Transmission input shaft

series of three fans inside a housing between engine and transmission. The first fan is driven directly by the engine. This fan stirs a hydraulic fluid into motion and increases the pressure of the fluid as engine speed increases. A second fan, attached to the input shaft of the transmission, is set spinning by the swirling fluid that surrounds it. Under low engine speeds — that is, when the engine is idling — the fluid transmits only a very small amount of power and motion to the drive train. This is what allows a car with automatic to idle in drive with very little forward motion, or "creep." The third fan is called the *stator*. The stator occupies an intermediate position. At low speeds it doesn't turn, but simply redirects the force of the hydraulic fluid from the driven fan back to the drive fan. At higher speeds, the stator begins to turn (a one-way clutch in the torque converter allows this to happen) as centrifugal force drives all three fans (and the fluid) together as if they were a solid mass.

Changing Gears in the Standard Transmission

Today's manually shifted cars have what is called a sliding-gear transmission with a progressive gear ratio. Working the shift lever on the floor or steering column causes the gears to slide in and out of mesh with each other, to provide different gear ratios necessary for efficient performance. In first gear, the engine can wind up to a higher speed, allowing a smooth start from a standing position without bucking or stalling.

Because of the ratio in first gear, it is impossible for the car to get up to road speed without racing the engine inefficiently at too high an rpm. Thus it is necessary to disengage the clutch and shift successively into the next higher gears.

This lets you get higher road speeds from slower engine rotation. In conventional transmissions, the final ratio in top gear — usually third or fourth — was one to one, meaning that each revolution of the crankshaft in the engine resulted in one revolution of the driveshaft. In response to increased concern over fuel economy, though, engineers have developed standard transmissions with *overdrive*, usually a fifth gear but sometimes applying to both fourth and fifth. In overdrive, the ratio actually exceeds one to one in favor of the driveshaft: it takes less than one revolution of the crankshaft to turn the driveshaft around once, so that the engine "loafs along" at highway speeds while burning small amounts of fuel.

As you engage and disengage the clutch and shift gears, internal transmission parts are subjected to a lot of friction and pressure. The wearing effects of these forces are eliminated by a supply of lubricant, which is usually somewhat heavier than the oil used in the engine. Cold temperatures thicken transmission oil considerably, which is why it sometimes takes three hands to get the shift lever to budge on a winter morning. To get around this problem, some manufacturers recommend replacing, or at least diluting, the transmission lubricant with a lower-viscosity oil during cold weather.

How the Automatic Shifts Gears

The automatic transmission has the same job to do as the standard — namely, to adjust gear ratios between the engine and drive train according to engine and road speeds. The first obvious difference between the two is that the automatic does this on its own, in response to changing engine speeds, and not at the driver's discretion. The automatic is not a sliding-gear transmission like the standard; it is a *planetary-gear* transmission. This means that the gears are engaged at all times, and that gear ratios are changed through the control of bands and clutches that

The Sliding Gear Transmission

Top view of transaxle, with
manual transmission

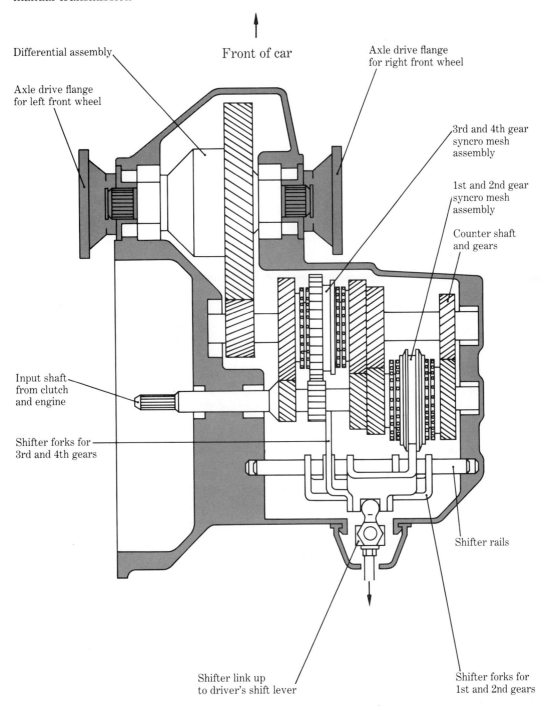

Front of car

Differential assembly

Axle drive flange
for left front wheel

Axle drive flange
for right front wheel

3rd and 4th gear
syncro mesh
assembly

1st and 2nd gear
syncro mesh
assembly

Counter shaft
and gears

Input shaft
from clutch
and engine

Shifter forks for
3rd and 4th gears

Shifter rails

Shifter link up
to driver's shift lever

Shifter forks for
1st and 2nd gears

The Automatic Transmission

*Confusing, isn't it? That's why
this is best left to a specialist!*

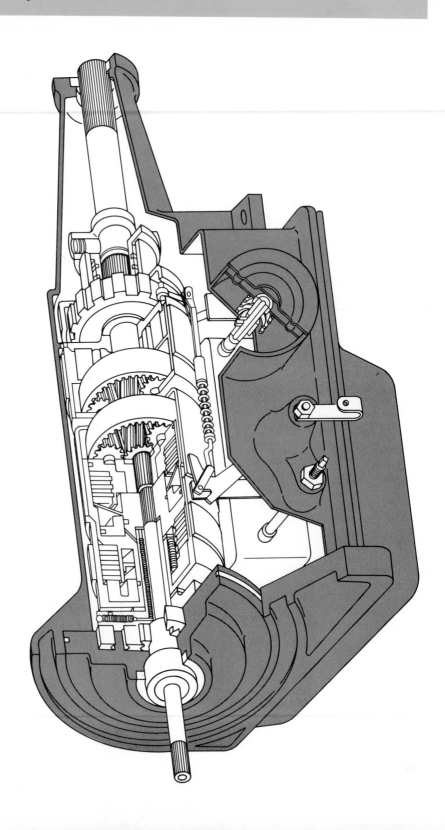

allow certain members of the planetary-gear train either to stop turning, turn backward, or turn at a different speed.

As we saw earlier, the connection between engine and transmission in the automatic is hydraulic rather than mechanical. The exception is late-model cars having what is called a *lock-up torque converter*. This involves a mechanical clutch that locks the input and output sides of the converter together in top gear (third or fourth, the overdrive gears). This improves fuel economy by eliminating slippage, which is characteristic of fluid drive and which tends to increase momentarily when the driver's foot comes down hard on the gas pedal at any speed.

The lock-up unit helps fuel economy, but there are some minor tradeoffs. One is occasional rough shifting: some cars with lock-up torque converters will shift in and out of the lock-up mode while the car is climbing moderate grades, leaving the driver with the impression that something is wrong with either the transmission or the engine. However, this is a normal condition.

Getting Power to the Drive Wheels

There are two options for translating the engine's power into forward or reverse motion of the car: front-wheel drive (fwd) or rear-wheel drive (rwd). Both are in use today. In rwd, the transmission delivers its power directly to the driveshaft, which is connected to a *differential* (also called the rear end) located at the center of the rear axle. Actually, it isn't quite that simple. Since the rear axle is "live" — it has to move up and down with the bumps of the road — the driveshaft has to move along with it. This is where the *universal joints* come in. The "u-joints," as they are often called, are located at each end of the driveshaft. The rear u-joint is bolted to the pinion shaft, which serves as the input for the differential.

The differential serves three purposes. First, it makes possible a 90-degree shift in the direction followed by the rotary motion in the drive train, so that power is sent to the two wheels. Second, it provides the proper gear ratio between the drive train and the wheels. This is determined by engine size and power, transmission type, tire size, and vehicle weight. In most cars, the drive ratio between drive train and wheels ranges between two to one and three to one, meaning that the driveshaft makes two to three revolutions for every revolution of the rear wheels. This is called the *final drive* ratio, or rear-axle ratio.

The third purpose of the differential is to allow one wheel to turn faster than the other, without locking or binding. This is necessary so that the car can turn corners smoothly. When a car corners, the outer wheel has to cover more distance than the inner wheel. If both wheels are rotating at the same speed, the inner wheel would drag on the pavement. This would be detrimental to both tire wear and handling. But the spider gears and pinion gears in the differential case enable the outer wheel to turn faster during a turn — in effect, they continually transmit a greater portion of the power to the wheel that is traveling the fastest.

That's the good news. But when one wheel is stuck in snow or mud, or on ice, and the other has a tighter grip on the road surface, guess which wheel gets the power? It's the wheel that spins most freely — namely, the one that's in trouble to begin with. Meanwhile, the wheel with the good surface beneath it might remain absolutely stationary.

Automotive engineers tackled this problem by developing a *positive traction differential*, sometimes known by the GM trade name of Positraction, or by the term equal-lock differential. These differentials employ clutches at each side of the axle shaft output. These clutches apply a given amount of pressure to each side of the axle, so that even if one wheel is on sheer

Getting Power to the Drive Wheels

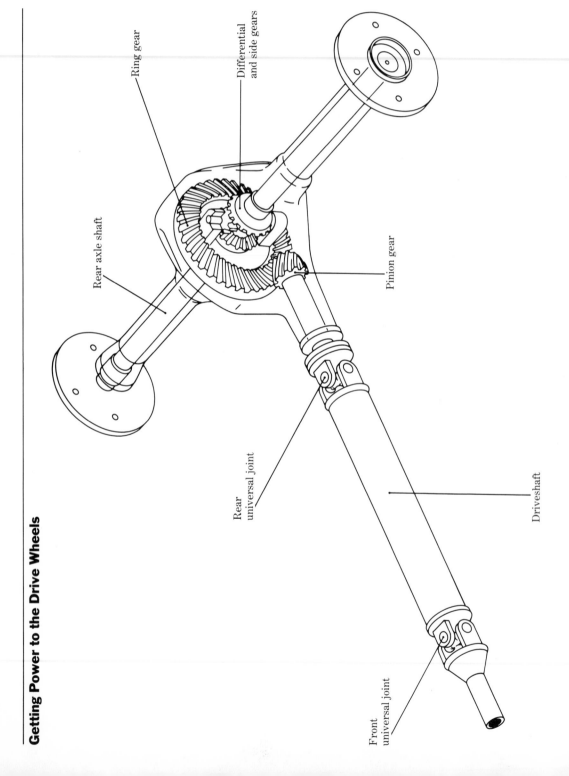

Ring gear

Differential
and side gears

Rear axle shaft

Pinion gear

Rear
universal joint

Driveshaft

Front
universal joint

ice, the other wheel will still receive a certain amount of power. This particular type of limited-slip differential, though, can only be used on rwd cars. If used with fwd, there would be too great an effect on steering.

Front-Wheel Drive

In a front-wheel-drive car, the drive train is shortened. The transmission output shaft is the input shaft of the differential. This transmission-differential combination, which is assembled as a single unit, is called a *transaxle*. At each end of the transaxle is a *half-shaft*, also called a "stub shaft," which delivers power to each of the front wheels. In most fwd cars (there are exceptions, including the Renault Fuego, Saab, Audi, and some small Toyotas), both the engine and the transaxle are mounted sideways in the engine compartment so that the rotary motion passing through the transaxle is already parallel to the wheels it must drive. With the fore-and-aft fwd engines, a more conventional differential is employed.

Even more than the rear axle, the front wheels have to be able to move freely as the car moves down the road. But the u-joint setup used at the driveshaft-differential connection in a rwd car won't work well with fwd. If simple u-joints were used between the transaxle outputs and the front wheels, there would be a slight pulsation in the drive mechanism when the steering wheel was turned sharply one way or the other and acceleration attempted. This is because u-joints do not transmit rotary motion absolutely smoothly. As they turn, there is a slight increase and decrease of velocity called *phasing*. This presents no problem in the rwd configuration, but would be unacceptable up front where steering and drive are focused at the same point.

Instead of u-joints, at the outer end of each fwd half-shaft is a device called a *constant-velocity joint*, or "cv joint." It is a more sophisticated (and more expensive) version of a u-joint that allows both vertical and lateral motion of the wheels. Actually, each cv joint is nothing more than two u-joints in one. These could be

Front-Wheel Drive

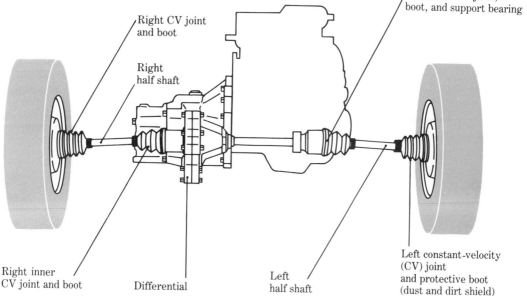

Right CV joint and boot

Right half shaft

Left inner CV joint, boot, and support bearing

Right inner CV joint and boot

Differential

Left half shaft

Left constant-velocity (CV) joint and protective boot (dust and dirt shield)

the cross-and-trunion type, like the ones used in rwd drive trains, or the somewhat more complicated ball-and-socket design. The complexity of the cv joint makes fwd cars more expensive to maintain — a factor that could cancel out any long-range savings on fuel that may be anticipated in a small fwd.

Drive-Train Maintenance

Much of the maintenance of an automobile's drive train is preventive, particularly with regard to the clutch. Clutches can be damaged in many different ways. One common bad habit is called "riding the clutch" — driving along with your foot resting lightly on the clutch pedal, as if it were a footstool. This keeps the throwout bearing constantly engaged with the clutch fork and pressure plate, causing the bearing to wear prematurely. What's more, the slight release in the tension of the pressure-plate springs resulting from this partial disengaging of the clutch can

cause the clutch to slip under heavy power application such as hill climbing or passing. If you have this habit, break it. Keep your foot firmly on the floor, away from the clutch pedal, unless you are shifting gears.

Drivers should also be aware of the approximately one inch of free play at the top of the pedal's path of travel. This can be felt as a moment of very slight resistance, with little spring tension, when you first put your foot down on the pedal. The purpose of this inch of free play is to keep the throwout bearing safely away from the operating levers on the pressure plate when the clutch is engaged. Otherwise, the pressure plate might not be able to keep the clutch disc firmly pressed against the flywheel, and the clutch would slip. The heat and friction of constant slippage wears the lining from the clutch plate. Once this happens, you're in for a clutch replacement.

Front-wheel Drive: Pros and Cons

Is the rush toward front-wheel drive necessarily a good thing? Actually, the technology has been around as long as autos have. The first powered vehicle, a steam tractor built in the 1760s, had front-wheel drive. Saab and Audi have always built their cars that way. It is all the rage today.

Like most automotive technologies, fwd has its pros and cons. It is undoubtedly agile in most driving circumstances, and the presence of the major weight of the car over the wheels helps to improve traction on snow-covered straightaways and inclines. Also, elimination of the drive train from beneath the passenger compartment enables manufacturers to

build small, lightweight, fuel-efficient cars that are still reasonably roomy. This is essential if federal fuel-economy requirements are to be met with a product still capable of selling to a wide market.

On the minus side, in addition to the increased pass-along engineering costs and higher repair bills fwd entails, there have been problems with weight distribution: when the weight shifts to the front of the car during a quick stop, the rear wheels may lock too soon, as happened with some of GM's X-cars. This can also happen in fwd cars that have automatic transmissions, since the front wheels, even when your foot is off the gas, are still receiving a small amount of power while the rear wheels aren't. In other words, the brakes could take less time to stop the car from the back than from the front.

Finally, there is the potential for "understeer" on hard-packed snow and ice, a phenomenon that can result when the front wheels are directed into a turn but the car still wants to go straight ahead. Saab, the veteran Swedish front-wheel-drive automaker, tells us to stay off the brake in this situation, let go of the gas, and steer into the skid in order to regain traction and direction.

Front- and rear-wheel drive will no doubt continue to coexist over the years, and engineering will correct some fwd faults. But the question remains: Why are some of the world's best-handling cars — such as BMW, Mercedes-Benz, Ferrari, Lamborghini, Maserati, Porsche — all rear-wheel drive?

So, check the amount of free play in your clutch pedal from time to time, using either your hand or foot. If there doesn't seem to be enough play, have your mechanic take a look at it and make whatever adjustments may be necessary.

Another thing *never* to do is to hold a car in place on a hill by letting the clutch out partway. In such a situation, you are deliberately inducing clutch slippage, along with all the damage it can do.

As you might suspect, any apparatus as dependent upon friction as an automobile clutch will suffer from misplaced, accidental lubrication. We're talking about what can happen when oil leaking from the rear main seal of the engine, or from the front seal of the transmission, finds its way onto the clutch plate. The clutch will slip and may even start to chatter.

Normally, "chattering" in a clutch is associated with a weakening of the tension in the takeup springs in the clutch disc. The disc is made up of two pieces held together with these springs. The outer piece has the lining, which makes contact with the pressure plate. The inner piece is the central hub, containing the spline that extends from the transmission. The takeup springs that hold the two pieces together absorb the initial shock of engagement with the spinning flywheel. If the tension in these springs is lost, the clutch will chatter and the whole car will begin to shake as you let up on the clutch pedal. The only remedy is clutch replacement, before serious damage is done to the entire drive train.

There's no need to lubricate any of the parts of a clutch, nor is there any way you can. The clutch is essentially a sealed unit, installed for the life of the car unless one of the above-mentioned problems leads to its demise. But with careful driving habits, a clutch may never need replacing. A 100,000-mile clutch lifespan is not uncommon, and there are even some city taxicabs — with all the stop-and-go driving they do — that have gone 200,000 miles on a single clutch.

The differential and rear axle require no regular maintenance other than a periodic fluid change in accordance with owner's manual recommendations. Like engine oil, the heavier lubricant in the differential can become contaminated with metal particles and moisture. Some car manufacturers advise that a lighter-viscosity lubricant be used in the differentials of cars driven in cold climates. If the rear-end lubricant is too heavy, it will remain a virtual solid during low-temperature operation, and the gears will "channel" right through it. These parts will thus not receive proper lubrication, and serious damage could result.

Drive-Train Brothers

Most people not associated with the auto industry credit Henry Ford with the invention of the automobile. While this is not true, the senior Ford did put his cars together using the first assembly lines. He also farmed work out. Among his suppliers were two brothers who built engines and transmissions to be installed in Ford cars on Ford assembly lines.

. The brothers, however, were ambitious, and decided that they, the producers of Ford's engines, could build just as good a car of their own. So, in 1919 Horace and John produced and built their first car with a name plate still seen today.

The name of these Ford-power-train-builders-turned-car-manufacturers? Horace and John Dodge.

The "Triple-S" Systems: Stopping, Steering, and Suspension

Braking

Most cars today use a combination of *disc* and *drum* brakes, with the disc brakes mounted in the front and the drum brakes in the rear. Although both of these approaches to braking use friction to stop the car, their operating mechanisms are substantially different.

In the drum braking system, two stationary, crescent-shaped brake "shoes" press outward against the inside of a rotating drum to provide the friction necessary to stop the car when the driver steps on the brake pedal. With disc brakes, a specially surfaced steel rotor turns with the wheel, which is stopped when two pads, mounted opposite each other with the rotor in between, press together and exert friction upon the rotor.

The brake pads are mounted onto devices called *brake calipers*, which are in turn attached to the suspension members of each front wheel (or to all four wheels, in the less-common case of four-wheel disc braking). The calipers are hydraulic devices operated by the pressurized brake fluid in the lines extending from the *master cylinder*. The pressure is created when the driver steps on the brake pedal.

There are two techniques used in applying braking pressure to the calipers and pads. In one, there is a piston on each side of the caliper, so that force is directly applied to both pads and consequently to both sides of the rotor. The other technique, employed on almost all American

Reverse Engines!

You take it for granted that your car will stop each time you step on the brakes, but if you were a normal driver in the 1920s and you purchased one of Henry Ford's Model T Tin Lizzies, you might have had to use reverse gear in the transmission to bring the car to a quick stop.

Cars of this vintage had brakes on the rear wheels only and were difficult to stop in an emergency. It was common practice for drivers of the Ford car to rely on the reverse-gear trick to help stop.

It wasn't until the late 1920s that four-wheel brakes and hydraulic brakes became accepted. Walter Chrysler put the hydraulic brake into the first mass-produced car in 1928. But Henry Ford, who is credited by some historians as being the most innovative man in the auto industry, would not let the hydraulic brake be used on his cars until 1939 (and would not use independent front suspension until 1949, fifteen years after the rest of the industry had adopted it).

Disc Brakes vs. Drum Brakes

Disc Brake

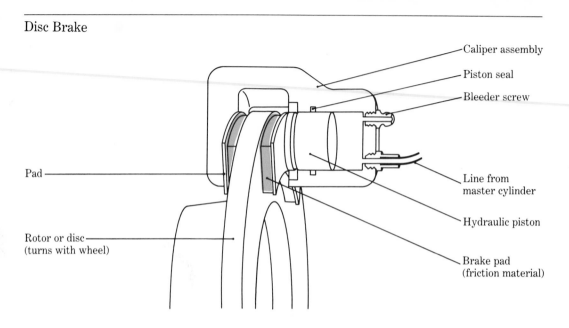

Caliper assembly

Piston seal

Bleeder screw

Pad

Line from
master cylinder

Hydraulic piston

Rotor or disc
(turns with wheel)

Brake pad
(friction material)

Drum Brake

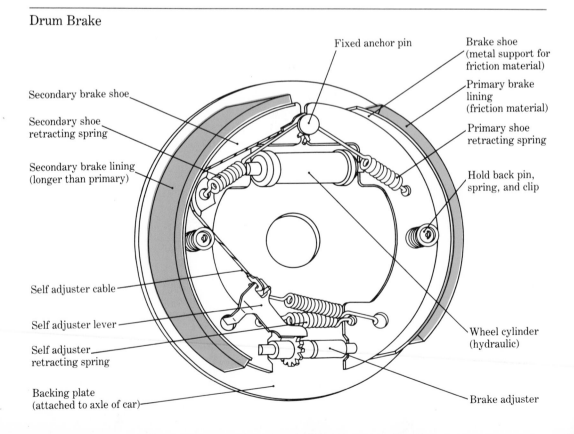

Fixed anchor pin

Brake shoe
(metal support for
friction material)

Secondary brake shoe

Primary brake
lining
(friction material)

Secondary shoe
retracting spring

Primary shoe
retracting spring

Secondary brake lining
(longer than primary)

Hold back pin,
spring, and clip

Self adjuster cable

Self adjuster lever

Self adjuster
retracting spring

Wheel cylinder
(hydraulic)

Backing plate
(attached to axle of car)

Brake adjuster

cars as well as most imports, is called the "floating caliper" disc brake. Here there is only one piston, which pushes one pad and pulls the other toward the rotor simultaneously.

Drum brakes, which before the advent of the discs were used on all four wheels, also operate hydraulically, using pressure from the driver's foot applied via the master cylinder. Mounted near the top of a stationary backing plate at each wheel is a hydraulic *wheel cylinder*, along with an anchor pin and the spring assembly to which the brake shoes are attached. There are pistons in the front and back of the wheel cylinder. When the driver steps on the brake pedal, the pistons push outward against the springs, which in turn force the shoes against the inside of the brake drum.

There are several reasons why disc brakes have taken over the drums, at least on the front wheels of most cars. One is the fact that the disc brakes employ a much smaller braking surface than their rear-wheel counterparts. This may seem paradoxical, but braking power is not simply proportional to the size of the surface to which friction is applied. For one thing, there is greater hydraulic pressure (usually provided in today's cars by a power assist) behind the disc pads; for another, the pads themselves have a harder surface than brake shoes. But most important of all, the smaller friction surface means that the rotor is more capable of dissipating heat during its revolutions than the drum-and-shoes assembly. In drum brakes, the shoes cover so much of the interior surface of the drums that there is very little time

The Brake Hydraulic System

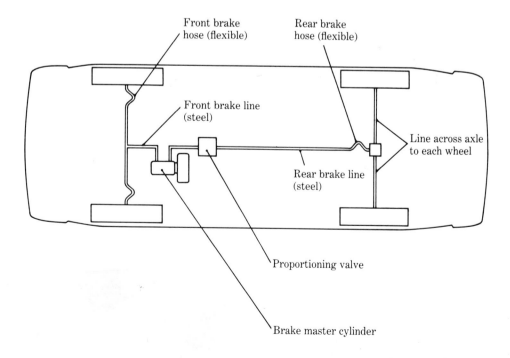

Front brake hose (flexible)

Rear brake hose (flexible)

Front brake line (steel)

Line across axle to each wheel

Rear brake line (steel)

Proportioning valve

Brake master cylinder

for heat to dissipate — and of course, tremendous amounts of heat result from braking friction. In cars using drum brakes exclusively, this led to a problem called *brake fade*, in which the shoes got so hot after repeated braking that their surfaces would glaze and provide very little friction against the drums. The brake pedal would go down, but the car wouldn't stop.

Another advantage of disc brakes is their relative imperviousness to water. In drum brakes, centrifugal force holds water inside the drum and reduces the friction between drum and shoes — you drive through a puddle, and your brakes suddenly become less effective. But the disc-brake rotor, spinning on the same plane as the wheel, tends to throw water off, providing a dry area of contact for the pads.

The calipers (front) and wheel cylinders (rear) are connected to the car's main steel brake lines by flexible lines, which allow the wheels to move up and down and, in the front, to steer without the lines breaking. The steel lines run to the master cylinder by way of an important component called the *proportioning valve*. In a combination disc-drum braking system, the proportioning valve allows for the difference in friction characteristics between the two modes by meting out the proper amount of pressure to front and

rear when the driver steps on the pedal. This prevents either set of wheels from locking before the car has come to a stop.

The proportioning valve has an especially important job to do on front-wheel-drive cars. When the brakes are applied hard in a car with fwd, the rear wheels have a tendency to lift — in some cases, they are only held to the road by 50 pounds of pressure. (The inside rear wheel of a Volkswagen Rabbit may actually leave the ground during hard cornering.) With this little downward pressure, the braking on the rear wheels has to be very gentle, or else they will lock and the car could become difficult to handle. It is the adjustment of the proportioning valve that regulates braking pressure and keeps this from happening. It was improper proportioning-valve adjustment, in fact, that caused the well-publicized spinout problems in 1979 and 1980 Chevrolet Citations. The rear wheels locked, and the car spun.

Since the proportioning valve is designed to "tailor" braking pressures for specific cars, it should go without saying that these valves are not interchangeable from car to car. Continued safe braking requires that *only* a valve designed for a particular model and year be used as a replacement part on a car of that model and year.

Following the brake system from the wheels back to the pedal and the driv-

Stop!

The brake systems on today's cars are built to provide some braking action even in the event of a rupture in part of the hydraulic brake lines. All cars built and sold in the United States since the late 1960s are required to have two separate

hydraulic systems so that if one should fail, the other will apply brakes on at least two wheels.

However, the brake pedal effort in this situation is increased, and you may even feel as if the brake pedal is all the way to the floor. Don't give up pushing, though — you still have some

braking power. But make a beeline to a repair station and have the problem corrected right away. You are not driving a Model T Ford and can't use reverse to stop the car.

Dual Diagonal vs. Front-to-Rear Brakes

Diagonally Split Two Circuit Brake System

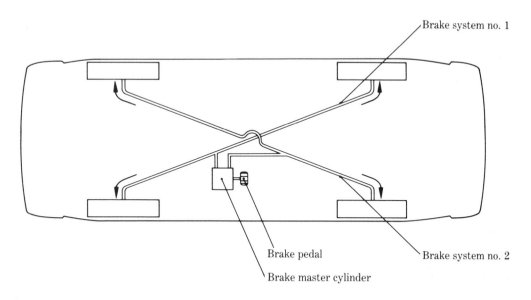

Brake system no. 1

Brake pedal

Brake master cylinder

Brake system no. 2

Two Circuit Front-to-Rear Hydraulic System

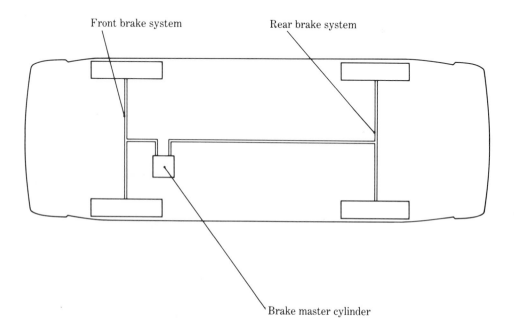

Front brake system

Rear brake system

Brake master cylinder

er's foot, we come to the focal point of braking hydraulics, the master cylinder. The master cylinder is a dual-stage device connected by mechanical linkage to the brake pedal. It is called "dual-stage" because one part operates the front brakes while the other part operates the rear, so that a failure of the braking system at either end of the car will leave stopping power at the other end unaffected. Some foreign cars use a "dual-diagonal" system, in which there are always three wheels with braking capability even if one line fails. In such cars there are four main brake lines rather than two, so that the necessary redundancy is provided.

Nowadays, the master cylinder is usually power-boosted, which lends the term "power brakes" to the braking systems on all but the smallest cars. There are two ways to provide this power assist. The first is the *vacuum* method, in which vacuum from the engine pulls down a diaphragm to increase the master cylinder's hydraulic pressure when the driver applies the brakes. This is the older approach to power braking, but it isn't as effective on today's smaller cars, which have less available engine vacuum. This consideration led to the development of the *hydraulic* booster, filled with pressurized fluid from the power-steering system of the car (driven by a fan belt). When the driver steps down on the pedal, it opens a valve that brings the pressure of this fluid to bear on the braking system.

The term "power brakes" might be more accurately changed to "power-*assisted*" brakes. If the power fails, the brakes are not rendered useless. It may take two feet to get the pedal to the floor, but there is still braking pressure available.

The Emergency Brake

On nearly all cars, the emergency brake (or *parking brake*) lever is connected to the rear drum brakes. It works by means of a mechanical linkage and cable, rather than hydraulics, but does the same job of expanding the brake shoes against the interior of the rear wheel drums.

There's one problem worth noting with regard to the drum-brake emergency system. Drum brakes work best in only one direction: forward. This is because they're built to operate on what is called the duo-servo action. "Duo-servo" is a fancy name for using the forward rotation of the wheel to help increase the pushing power of the shoes against the drum. The front shoe thus becomes a reactor, picking up the rotation of the drum and pushing it against the rear shoe, which then presses all the harder against the drum. (The rear brake shoe can't rotate along with the drum, because it is held in place by the anchor pin at the top of the backing plate.) Because of the duo-servo action, it's necessary to pull up a bit harder on the emergency brake lever when you park a car

Parking on a Hill

People worry about the effects of outside sources of energy on the transmissions of their cars. Some are particularly concerned about the effects of parking on hills.

The automatic transmissions of today's cars are designed to withstand hill parking. Of course, it is always advisable to use the emergency brake when parking in any situation. When parking on a hill, the front wheels can also be used as parking aids. To do this, simply turn the wheels in toward the curb on the downhill side, so that should the car break loose and roll, the wheel closest to the curb will stop it. Some people like to turn the wheels in and let the car roll until the wheel just touches the curb when parking. This practice cannot be recommended without qualification, as it tends to knock the front end out of alignment if not done carefully.

Just remember to turn the wheels away from the curb before driving away, or you will surely force the front end out of alignment. This will, in turn, adversely affect tire wear and handling.

with the rear end pointing down a hill than when it is pointing front-end down.

Braking System Maintenance

Depending on the car and the type of driving done, disc brakes should be overhauled every 30,000 to 50,000 miles. An overhaul involves replacement of the pads, which eventually lose most of their special friction surface, and often a turning of the rotor on a lathe for resurfacing. Shoes on drum brakes must also be replaced, although when they are serving the rear wheels only they will generally last longer than the front discs.

When disc brakes are overhauled, the calipers should also be examined to make sure they are not sticking and holding the pads in contact with the rotor. The drag induced by this type of caliper failure can reduce gas mileage, cause premature wearing of the pads, and pull the car to one side or the other, making steering difficult. Wheel cylinders on drum brakes should also be checked for free play.

Finally, don't forget the flexible brake lines, which can deteriorate with time and leak fluid. Check the lines when performing brake service, and also check the level of the brake fluid in its reservoir.

Steering

There are several different types of steering systems in use on modern automobiles — power and manual, gearbox, and rack-and-pinion — but we can start out with at least one simple generality: all cars have front-wheel steering. The only possible exceptions are a handful of experimental three-wheelers, which are steered by moving the single back wheel. These need

The Gearbox (or Parallelogram) Steering System

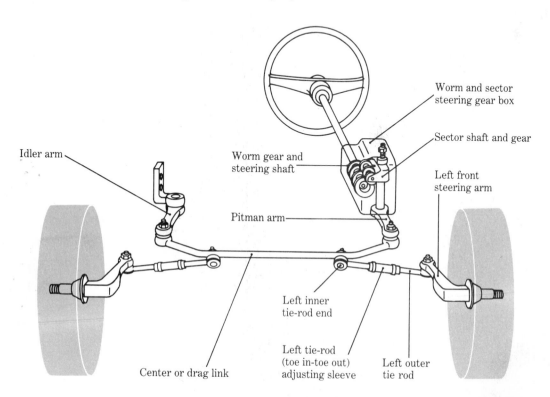

Worm and sector steering gear box

Sector shaft and gear

Left front steering arm

Worm gear and steering shaft

Idler arm

Pitman arm

Left inner tie-rod end

Left tie-rod (toe in-toe out) adjusting sleeve

Left outer tie rod

Center or drag link

not concern us here. There are times when tight parking spaces might make us wish that all four wheels could be steered, but this would be sheer disaster on the open road. So, let's get down to those two front wheels and how we move them left and right.

The parts of the steering system we are most familiar with are the steering wheel and column, which are, of course, located inside the passenger compartment. The steering column extends up through the firewall and is a descendant of the early straight columns atop which sat a simple steering tiller. The operation of the wheel needs no explanation, but things get a little more complicated at the other end of the column. We'll start with the conventional gearbox steering arrangement, which, until the recent wider acceptance of rack-and-pinion, was the standard

steering aparatus and still predominates among American cars.

The steering gearbox contains a *worm gear* at the end of the steering column. The worm gear, which resembles the threading on a screw, meshes with a *sector gear* connected through the sector shaft to a *Pitman arm*. When the wheel is turned, motion is transferred through each component of this apparatus to the steering linkage to direct the wheels to the left or right. (We'll take a more detailed look at that linkage later.)

The rack-and-pinion system, which has been perfected over many years by European manufacturers, works somewhat differently. Instead of a worm gear, this system calls for a square-cut gear at the end of the steering column. This gear meshes with a *rack*, which is simply a length of steel with teeth cut into it. Turning the steering wheel thus makes the

The Rack-and-Pinion Steering System

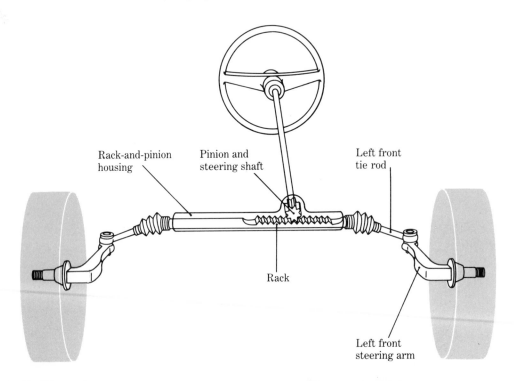

Rack-and-pinion housing

Pinion and steering shaft

Left front tie rod

Rack

Left front steering arm

rack move to the left or right. The steering linkage can be connected to either end of the rack.

Many car enthusiasts claim that the rack-and-pinion system is more responsive, providing better "road feel" than its gearbox counterpart. Its greatest advantage, however, is its light weight, resulting from the elimination of the heavy gearbox, and the relative ease with which it can be produced.

Power Steering

Either rack-and-pinion or gearbox steering mechanisms can be adapted to receive power assist, or what we usually call *power steering*. On front-wheel-drive cars, and on heavier rear-wheel-drive models, power steering is usually the norm today. Its usefulness with front-wheel drive stems from the tendency of fwd to feed some power impulses back into the steering wheel; power steering provides some insulation from this and gives the car a smoother feel. Some smaller front-wheel-drive cars work perfectly well, though, without power steering, as do many lighter cars with rear-wheel-drive.

The power steering apparatus is a series of hydraulic pistons, built into either the steering gearbox or the rack-and-pinion mechanism. The hydraulic pressure to operate the pistons comes from a pump mounted on the front of the engine and driven by a fan belt. The control valves regulating the hydraulic pressure are usually located either in the steering gearbox or at the point of contact between the rack and steering column, and are pressure-sensitive to the driver's touch. If the driver has the car pointing straight down the road, very little pressure is applied to the power steering apparatus. But when the wheel is turned to the left or right, the control valves sense the pull and apply hydraulic pressure to assist the driver in turning the wheel.

A recent innovation has been variable power steering, in which the amount of assistance is in inverse proportion to the speed of the car. When you're elbowing into a parking space, the system offers maximum assistance; when you're at highway speeds, power assist is minimal. This is ideal, since too much input from power steering on the open road results in a "mushy," imprecise feeling in the wheel.

The Steering Linkage

In cars with gearbox steering, the normal method of transmitting motion to the wheels is through a system of links called *parallelogram* steering, after the shape described by the principal components of the linkage. The motion transferred from the sector gear and shaft to the Pitman arm is in turn applied to the *center link*, also called the *relay rod*.

All this is happening on the driver's side of the car, where the steering gearbox is located. On the opposite side, the relay rod is connected at a pivot point to the *idler arm*, which parallels the Pitman arm and duplicates its motions. (Many drivers will be familiar with the idler arm at least by name, since it commonly requires replacement because of wearing and loosening.) Working together on their respective pivot points, the Pitman arm and idler arm cause the relay rod to move from side to side and thus to direct the steering of the car.

Extending from the relay rod to the wheels on both sides are two *tie rods*. On each end of the tie rods are ball-and-socket joints called *tie-rod ends*. Each tie rod has both an inner and an outer tie-rod end. The tie-rod ends are attached to the *steering arms*, which complete the system and cause the wheels to turn.

To help the wheel pivot from left to right, and to integrate the steering system with the car's suspension, there are upper and lower ball joints (if the car is so equipped) and king pins, or the lower ball joint and MacPherson strut arrangement, which we'll learn about in the concluding part of this chapter.

On cars with rack-and-pinion steering, the rack itself takes the place of the relay rod and idler arm. The tie rods are simply connected to the opposite ends of the rack, either with inner and outer tie-rod ends, or with outer tie-rod ends and a ball-and-socket joint on the end of the rack itself. The simplicity of this arrangement should make it easy to see why rack-and-pinion has its staunch advocates, at least for small, light, performance cars: with fewer parts, there's less wasted motion, and the steering and road feel are likely to be more precise.

The Suspension System

In basic terms, the suspension system is what keeps the body (and passengers) of the car from having to absorb every jounce in the road, and enables the driver to handle the car comfortably and securely. Suspension systems are complicated and vary greatly in today's cars, ranging all the way from models with solid axles front and rear, to those with independent four-wheel suspension. Regardless of how they are put together, though, there are certain elements of automobile suspension used throughout the industry that may be discussed generically even if they do not appear in every car model.

You can't have suspension without some type of *springs*. They are the first line of defense against the bumps in the road. There are three types of springs used on today's cars: *leaf* springs, *coil* springs, and *torsion bars*. The leaf spring is commonly found on heavy-duty trucks, and on the rear of cars having a "live" rear axle — that is, a single-piece axle incorporating the differential. As the name implies, this spring is made up of a series of steel "leaves" bolted together in the middle and having a pivot point at each end. It flattens and expands in length as it is compressed, and then rebounds to its original arched shape. The coil spring is what most of us would think of when the word "spring" is mentioned; it is simply a length of steel coiled to compress and expand in response to road-surface pressures. The torsion bar might best be explained as a coil spring that hasn't been coiled. Mounted laterally between two wheels, the bar is fixed firmly to the frame at one side, and at the other side is connected to the wheel by a lever. When the wheel moves up and down, so does the lever. The motion it imparts to the bar causes the bar to twist, thus providing suspension for the car.

There are many different ways of mounting springs. The mounting method used on the front ends of most domestic cars, and on many imports as well, involves coil springs in an arrangement called *long arm–short arm suspension*. Here two A-frame devices, the upper and lower control arms, are mounted to pivot points on the chassis. The upper control arm is shorter than the lower. To connect the outer ends of the two control arms, there are upper and lower *ball joints*. Between the two ball joints is the *steering-knuckle-and-spindle assembly*. Extending at a right angle from the steering knuckle, which connects the two ball joints, is the spindle, to which the *wheel* is attached. (The spindle is usually perpendicular with the road, with the wheel affixed to it at a right angle.) From either the back or front of the steering knuckle, the *steering arm* extends to the outer tie-rod end, as was described earlier. The steering knuckle is able to move back and forth as well as up and down, so that both suspension movement and steering capability are provided.

The coil spring in this arrangement could be mounted on either the upper or lower control arm. If it is mounted on the upper control arm, it extends upward to a specially reinforced part of the body that acts as the spring seat. As the upper control arm is pushed up by the wheel, it exerts pressure against the spring and thus holds the car up. If the spring is mounted on the lower control arm, it extends instead to a special point on the car's frame.

Suspension

Torsion Bar

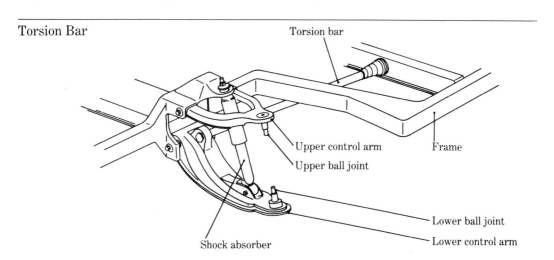

Coil Spring

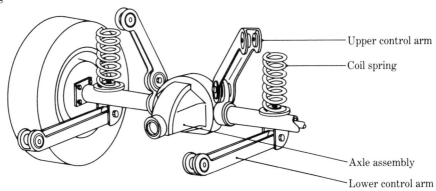

Leaf Spring

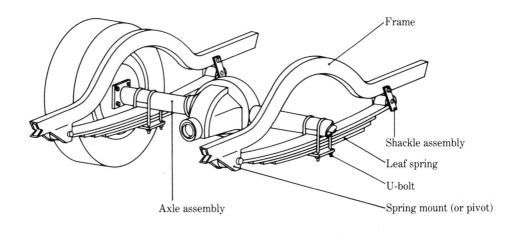

On the rear of the car (assuming a solid or "live" axle), the axle is mounted to the frame by means of *trailing arms* or *links*. These hold the axle in alignment with the car's frame, so that the rear wheels remain directly behind the front wheels and the car does not "crab" from side to side down the highway. At the same time, they allow the axle to move up and down with the action of the springs. The springs themselves are mounted at one end either on the trailing arms or on the axle assembly, and at the other, on the car's body or frame.

If leaf springs are used in the rear suspension, they are bolted to the rear axle assembly itself. The front pivot point (or "eye") of the leaf spring is secured to the car's frame, thus locating the axle relative to the frame. At the rear of the spring, though, there has to be some leeway. Here there is a *shackle*, or a double-pivot link. The shackle allows the spring to change its length as it flexes, while still

remaining securely attached to the frame. If the connection with the frame were rigid at both ends, the spring would either not compress and do its job, or break when pressure was exerted.

Enter the MacPherson Strut

Automobile springs and overall suspension remained pretty much the same for years. But as cars got smaller, and technology turned toward weight reduction as a means of improving fuel economy, something called the *MacPherson strut* came along to challenge the traditional front-end arrangement. MacPhersons were at one time found exclusively in European cars but now have come to be employed in many domestic models as well. Since the struts take the place of a number of conventional parts, they improve manufacturing efficiency and also cut back on

---

Suspension

Conventional Long Arm/
Short Arm Suspension

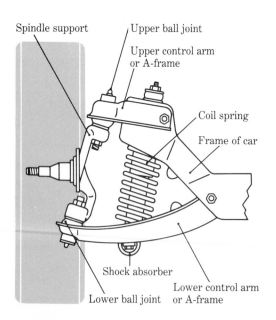

Spindle support   Upper ball joint

Upper control arm
or A-frame

Coil spring

Frame of car

Shock absorber

Lower ball joint   Lower control arm
or A-frame

The MacPherson Strut

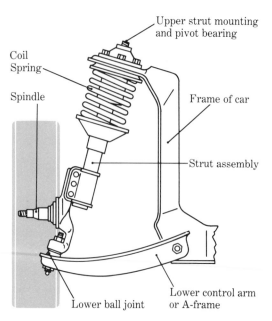

Upper strut mounting
and pivot bearing

Coil
Spring

Spindle

Frame of car

Strut assembly

Lower ball joint   Lower control arm
or A-frame

complexity and weight. They are a boon to small cars, and to cars with front-wheel drive.

Although it is used in conjunction with the lower control arm and lower ball joint, the MacPherson strut does away with the upper control arm and ball joint and builds the pivot point into the steering knuckle. The strut itself is a tubular, telescoping device that incorporates a spring, spindle support, and shock-absorber cartridge. The top of the strut is mounted on the car's frame, in the engine compartment, at a pivot point, which enables the car to be steered. At the lower end, there is a direct attachment to the steering arm.

The MacPherson strut is a modular component in which all of the above-mentioned suspension functions are combined.

The Shock Absorber

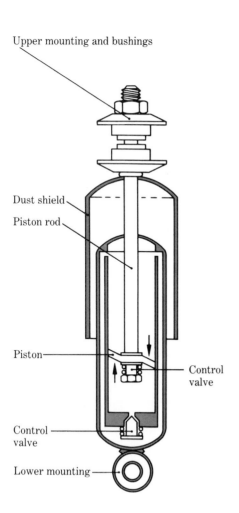

Upper mounting and bushings

Dust shield

Piston rod

Piston

Control valve

Control valve

Lower mounting

The MacPherson Strut

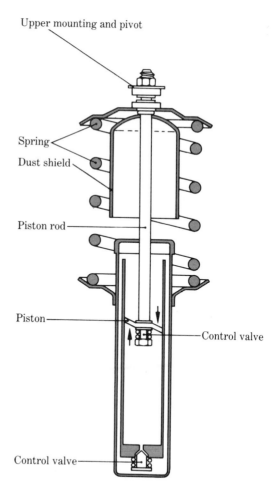

Upper mounting and pivot

Spring

Dust shield

Piston rod

Piston

Control valve

Control valve

But the reduction of weight this combination affords is necessarily balanced by added expense when it comes time to replace the struts. They are not cheap — a strut-replacement job on most cars will cost between $100 and $200, as compared to the $30 or so that it would cost to replace shock absorbers on a car with conventional front suspension. Good struts, however, will usually last longer than most shock absorbers.

Shock Absorbers

Springs, of course, are supposed to bounce, but if left to themselves, they would bounce too much, and the passengers in the car would feel as if they were riding in a boat. To prevent this, the rear ends of all cars and the front ends of cars without MacPherson struts employ *shock absorbers*, tubular hydraulic devices that dampen the compressing and rebounding action of the springs, making them work more slowly by absorbing some of the energies that make them bounce.

Actually, passenger seasickness isn't the half of what would happen on a car without shocks, or on a car with shocks that had badly deteriorated. They are essential to proper handling, since they keep the steering and suspension from having a mushy, wandering quality. And they are an absolute must for safety, since they keep the wheels on the road when the car goes over a bump. You can't steer, you can't accelerate, and you can't stop a car unless its wheels are firmly in contact with the road.

Shock absorbers also have a major effect on tire wear, a fact that can sometimes be overlooked even by otherwise conscientious front-end mechanics when they are diagnosing tire problems. If a shock absorber allows a wheel to move up and down excessively each time the car goes over a bump, there will be *camber* and *caster* changes, meaning that the wheel tilts either in and out or forward and backward, putting the tire in a variety of different contact angles to the road surface and wearing off its outer edges. If the shock absorber is so badly worn that it lets the tire leave the road, the tire will lose speed as it goes up in the air and scuff against the pavement when it comes down, much like an airplane tire during landing. The result will be a tire worn in spots and no longer completely round.

A car's original shocks begin to deteriorate at about 20,000 miles, and they do it gradually. Most drivers won't even notice how bad their shocks have gotten until a passenger points out how much the car bounces and floats. What happens to shocks as they age? The most common problem is that the upper seals fail, allowing small amounts of air to leak into the hydraulic fluid chamber. When this happens, the fluid foams. This thwarts the valving within the shock, which in modern double-acting hydraulic shocks allows different amounts of pressure to be exerted on the downward stroke and the rebound so that the spring motion can be dampened in both directions. With air-foamed fluid going through the valves, the action of the shock could become either harder or softer than was originally intended.

What should you look for when you buy replacement shocks? To begin with, the valving in the shocks should be calibrated to the car's original specifications, unless you know what you're doing and wish to have a firmer damping action for performance purposes. Also, you may want to look into the new gas-pressure shock absorbers. Each of these has a container of pressurized inert gas, kept separate from the fluid, which keeps pressure on the fluid at all times. Even if there is a slight leakage of air into the shock, the gas in its flexible container continues to expand, thus keeping the hydraulic fluid from foaming. Gas-pressure shock absorbers perform better even than brand-new conventional shocks and are now being used on such higher-priced American cars as Lincolns and Chrysler E and K LeBaron models.

Wheel Alignment

Camber (viewed from front of car)

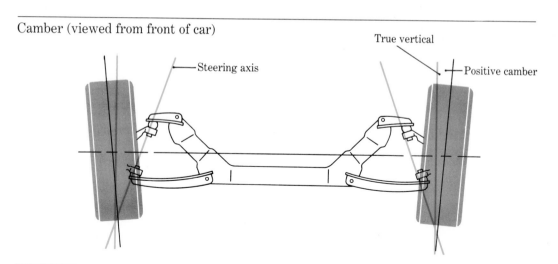

Toe in (viewed from top of car)

*Distance "A" is greater than
distance "B"*

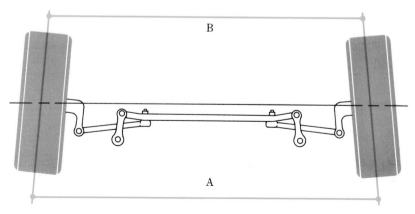

Caster (viewed from side of car)

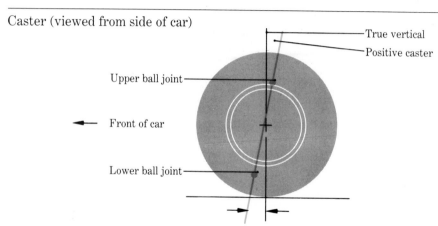

A Checklist for Good Maintenance

Proper car care does not have to consume all that much time and attention. By following a few simple, routine procedures, you can effectively increase the lifetime — in years and in mileage — that you can expect to get out of that expensive set of wheels you drive.

The following is a simple chart that categorizes necessary service operations according to mileage, time intervals, and seasons. Each listing is divided into two columns — one for the normal driver, and the second for those of us who give our cars "severe service." Most of us think we belong in the first group, but in reality we are often very hard on our cars. Most car makers list in their owner's manuals a special set of definitions of "severe service." These definitions nearly always include the following:

1   Frequent trips of less than 10 miles
2   Regular driving in a climate where the average temperature stays below 10°F for 60 days
3   High-speed driving in hot climates
4   Trailer towing
5   Stop-and-go driving

To this list, we might add:

6   Driving in dusty conditions. This does not have to mean a sandstorm in the Sahara Desert. Driving in the northern United States during the winter, when the roads are covered with sand and salt, constitutes dusty conditions.
7   High humidity. Engines breathe as they run; if the air they breathe is heavily laden with moisture, the engine oil will become contaminated.

Perhaps an engine's worst enemy is short-trip driving in cold weather. In order to get an engine started in the cold, it is necessary to feed it a very rich mixture of fuel and air. The engine cannot possibly burn off all of this gasoline, though, and some of it makes its way out of the tailpipe.

But that's not the end of the story. A lot of the gasoline, in liquid form, slips down past the piston rings and mixes with the engine oil. This is a bad situation, since gasoline is not a lubricant, and it will ruin the lubricating properties of the oil. Unfortunately, checking the dipstick will give you no clue as to whether this is going on. The dipstick may tell you the crankcase is full. What it does not tell you is that the contents may be two-thirds oil and one-third gasoline.

Routine Inspection Procedures

During regular chassis lubrication, the car goes up on a lift. While it's up there, it is hoped that the person doing the job will take time to inspect the following:

1   Front end for looseness
2   Steering linkage
3   Shock absorbers
4   Hydraulic brake parts for leaks
5   Engine and transmission for oil leaks
6   Exhaust system for damage and holes
7   Springs
8   Fuel tank and lines
9   Frame and floorboard for rust
10   Emergency brake components
11   Tires and wheels
12   Wear on the disc brake pads (On some cars these are visible without dismantling the brake assembly.)

Once the car is back on the ground, a complete engine-compartment check and servicing should follow. This includes all of the following:

1   Hood latches and hinges
2   Cooling system and hoses
3   Air filter
4   Fan belt

5   All fluids:
  • power steering
  • coolant
  • windshield washer
  • transmission (if automatic)
  • brake fluid
  • battery water
6   All wiring for loose connections and frayed insulation
7   All vacuum lines
8   Fuel lines for leaks
9   Visual check of ignition system

A Checklist for Auto Maintenance

By system: when to clean, check, or replace parts, according to season of the year and age of the car

System	Mileage	
	Normal use	*Hard use*
Battery and Charging System		
Electronic Ignition System	See owner's manual	Check at same time as spark plugs
Point Ignition System	See owner's manual	Check dwell and timing every 5,000 miles. Replace points every 10,000 miles
Spark Plugs	Replace at 15,000 to 30,000 miles: see owner's manual	Check between 3,000 and 5,000 miles and replace as needed
Spark Plug Wires, Distributor Cap, and Rotor	Check at each spark plug service interval and replace as needed	
Air Filter	15,000 to 30,000 miles: see owner's manual	Check at each oil change and replace as needed
Chassis Lubrication (including under chassis for wear and safety. Also includes body lubrication)	7,000 to 15,000 miles: see owner's manual	3,000 miles

This under-hood check should not only be undertaken when the car is in the garage for service but should be a part of your Saturday morning routine. Remember that with the advent of self-service gas stations, the days of station attendants opening the hood and doing these things for us are fading fast. Unless we get the job done ourselves, neglect can lead to serious damage. Not only could this be costly; it could lead to a breakdown at 2:00 A.M. in the middle of nowhere.

Does car care pay? Ask Jack Borden, a former newsman for Channel 4 in Boston. Borden's 1971 Dodge just underwent body surgery at a local vocational school. The car has over 350,000 miles on the clock and has seen few repairs. In fact, the engine has never been apart. Bordon's secret? Maintenance!

Make it your secret too. Follow the procedures suggested in the chart below — for even better results, follow the "severe conditions" recommendations — and you too could lead a long, happy life with the same car.

Time

Normal use	Hard use
Check water in battery, and fan belt and condition of wiring once a month	
3 months to one year: see owner's manual	60 to 90 days

Season

Normal	Severe conditions
Test in spring and fall and repair or replace as needed	
	Check in spring and fall
Check in spring and fall	Replace in spring and fall
Replace each fall to insure better winter starting	
Service at each tuneup interval	
	At least in spring and fall, and after driving on sloppy, dusty, or salt-covered roads

Maintenance (cont.)

System	Mileage	
	Normal use	*Hard use*
Cooling System		
Emission Components	Check at each spark plug service interval, or see owner's manual	
Fuel Filter	See owner's manual	10,000 miles
Oil Change	7,000 to 15,000 miles: see owner's manual	3,000 miles
Oil Filter	Change with each oil change	
Positive Crankcase Ventilator Valve	Check at each oil change and replace as needed	
Automatic Transmission	Most cars recommend no service; see owner's manual	12,000 to 15,000 miles
Repack Front Wheel Bearings (in rear-wheel-drive cars)	10,000 to 30,000 miles: see owner's manual	10,000 miles
Brakes	Check at each lubrication. Replace when lining is between 60 and 75% worn. Drain and flush brake fluid once a year	
Front-End Alignment	12,000 to 15,000 miles	5,000 to 12,000 miles
Tire Rotation and Wheel Balance	5,000 to 10,000 miles	
Body (Exterior) Finish	Wash weekly, and polish and wax twice a year	
Wiper Blades		

Time

Normal use	Hard use
Inspect cooling system at each oil change. Replace coolant every 24 months. Check hoses, belts, and thermostat and replace as needed	Replace coolant every 12 months and check all components; replace as needed
	2 times a year
3 months to one year: see owner's manual	60 to 90 days
	Once a year
	Once a year

Season

Normal	Severe conditions
Check coolant level and antifreeze protection in spring and fall, and replenish as needed	
Spring and fall	
	Change oil to match viscosity to temperature
	Each spring
	Each spring
At least each spring and fall to correct the effects of potholes	
Spring and fall at snow-tire change time	
Replace in spring and fall, or when vision is hampered	

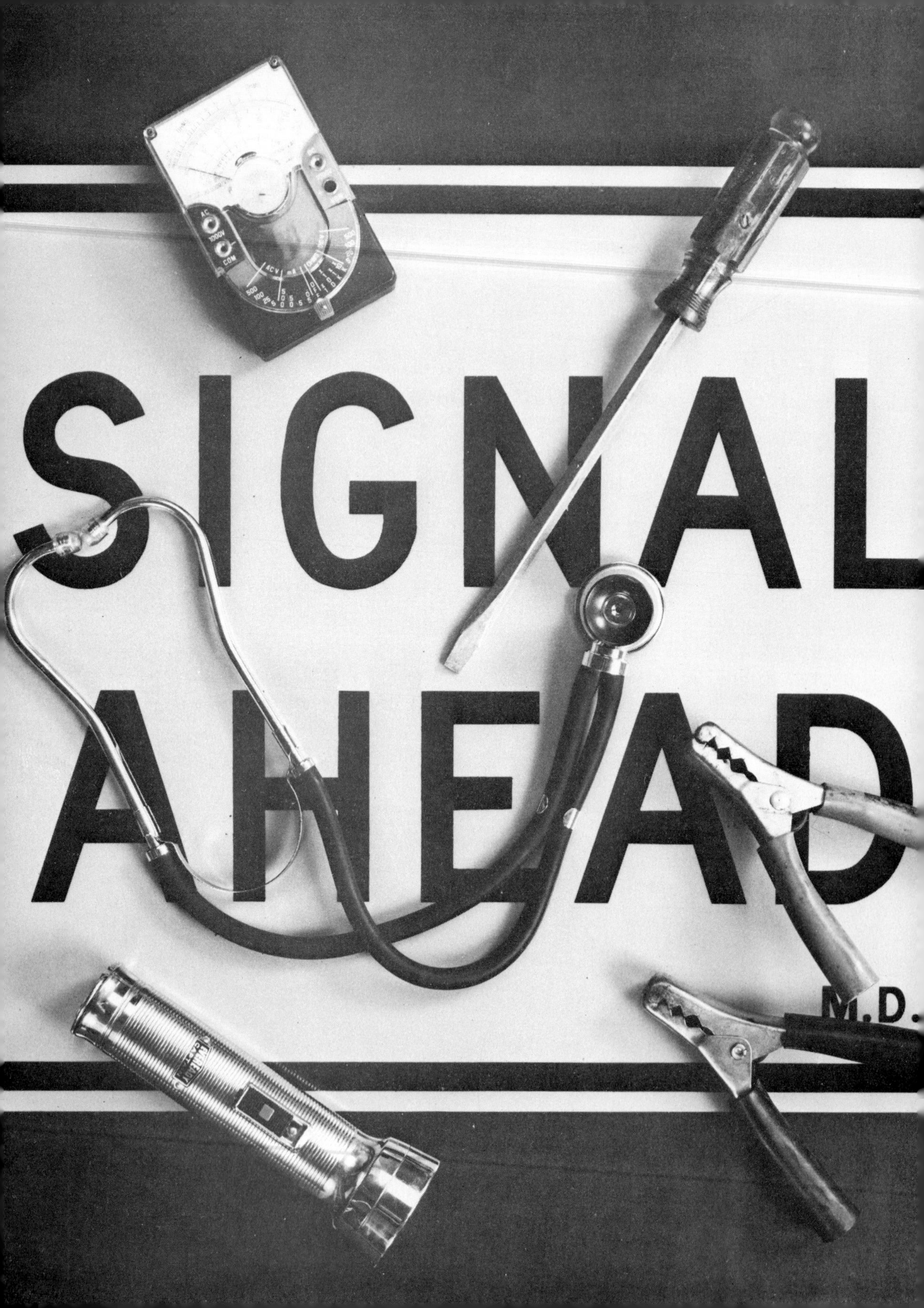
SIGNAL
AHEAD
M.D.

Troubleshooting: Listen to What Your Car Has to Say

Cars are more intelligent than most people think. For one thing, they have a way of letting us know when things aren't going just right. The signals are many and varied: clinks, pings, grinding noises, bumps and shudders, pulling to one side during braking or steering. Our responses to this assortment of warnings (early or otherwise) in turn help establish just how intelligent we are as drivers and determine whether our troubles will be big or small.

All too often, we drive for week after week with the windows rolled up, the air conditioner or heater fan humming, and the stereo turned up loud, oblivious of the sounds and other sensations that accompany common mechanical problems. We only sit up and take notice when some major trauma is already upon us, and it's too late to do anything but write large checks to the repairman. At least once a week, turn off the accessories, roll down the window, and *listen:* your car might be trying to tell you something, and it may be urgent.

Three Kinds of Diagnosis

There are three levels of automotive diagnosis. The first level, which we are alluding to here and which will occupy us in this chapter, consists of all those conclusions a layman can draw using his own five senses. The second level is that of a trained and competent mechanic, using his experience to decipher the signals that present themselves during road testing or close examination. Finally, there is the level of diagnosis that can be achieved only by a good mechanic using sophisticated electronic equipment. But the first line of defense is the driver, without whose close attention the mechanic and his equipment might not be called in until things have gone from bad to worse.

How do you know when something doesn't sound, smell, look, or feel the way it should? Start when your car is brand new, or just after a checkup or repair when your mechanic has assured you that everything is working properly. Then memorize as many details as you can: the feel of the ride, the sound of the engine; shifting, braking, and handling; the appearance of the various fluids. This way, you'll have a set of standards against which to measure later variations.

A Whimper, Not a Bang

Many car problems sneak up slowly and subtly. One example is the deterioration of shock absorbers, which can start at anywhere between 20,000 and 40,000 miles. If you drive the car every day, you aren't likely to notice the incremental changes in the ride — until a passenger gets in and asks how come your car feels like a boat in heavy seas, or until you happen to drive a car with new shocks and can see the difference for yourself. It's a similar story with tuneups. The erosion of performance and fuel economy caused by the wear of plugs and points may be hard to observe from day to day, but it's taking place nonetheless. Perhaps the best way to keep an eye on the situation is to maintain a mileage log. When the log shows that the number of miles you are getting out of each gallon of gas is beginning to slip, then you know it's time for a tuneup.

Keeping a good log can actually help you get away from the old idea that tuneup intervals must be governed by an inflexible schedule of mileage intervals. As long as the log shows that fuel economy is what it should be, and as long as the car starts well and runs smoothly, you can leave well enough alone. If not, or if cold weather or a long trip lies ahead, it's time to have a good mechanic check the engine with an electronic analyzer to determine which components might need to be replaced. This idea of analyzing and servicing *as the car needs it* makes a lot more sense than the old "blanket tuneup," and will help keep you from getting charged for tuneups that might not really have been performed.

Sounds, Smells, and Shimmies

Of course, you can't keep track of the whole picture just by using your calculator. There are a variety of sounds that, if you listen for them, can tell you what's going on (or going wrong) in the engine and the units attached to it: the water pump, power-steering pump, alternator, and other devices that turn on bearings. A common sound to listen for is a grinding noise, usually varying in pitch according to engine speed. There's a trick you can use to isolate this type of noise, and all it involves is a length of heater hose or garden hose. Open the hood while the engine is running, and place one end of the hose against the component you think may be causing the trouble. Put the other end to your ear. (You may have to test several different units; be careful when positioning the hose, as the fan and belts are unforgiving when it comes to stray fingers.) When you find the offending piece of machinery, the sound will come up through the hose as if it were a doctor's stethoscope. Then, you can tell your mechanic that you think you have a noisy water pump, or alternator, or whatever,

and that he should begin his own process of diagnosis with that part.

The engine itself can be the source of other telltale noises. A ticking sound that varies with engine speed could be associated with the hydraulic lifters, tappets, wrist pins, rings, connecting rods, or main bearings. Any such varying noise is a sign that the car should be brought in *immediately* for professional diagnosis. If caught early enough, problems with most of the above components can be corrected without the need for major surgery on the engine. For instance, you can often have a valve lifter or a camshaft replaced for $400 or $500, while a major overhaul necessitated by ignoring advance warnings might set you back $1500 to $2500. If the car is a few years old, this may mean the difference between the highway and the junkyard.

The diagnosis and repair of serious engine problems are beyond the scope of the average owner. But remember: if you hear a strange tick, and it varies with engine speed, have a mechanic look at the car right away.

It's easy to check the condition of your engine coolant. Shut the engine off and let it cool. Open the hood and, when the engine has cooled sufficiently, carefully remove the radiator cap and take a look at the coolant. First check the level, then the quality. The antifreeze or antifreeze and water should be clear, not dirty or muddy. If it is dirty, it may already have done damage to the cooling system. Ethylene glycol — the substance most commonly used as antifreeze — has a neutral base when it is fresh, but with the repeated heating and cooling that come with normal use, the base changes to acid. This can rapidly increase the corrosion of the system's metal parts.

Smell the antifreeze. It should have a sweet aroma; if it smells acrid, or acidy, it's time for flushing and replacement. It's a good idea to change the coolant every year in any event, preferably in the fall or spring before the arrival of harsh driving weather.

The next step in your fluids check is to pull the engine oil dipstick. The oil should be clean and somewhat translucent, with no sign of rust, foam, or other extraneous gunk on the stick above the oil-level mark. These are all indications that water has gotten into the crankcase — not from the cooling system, but from the outside environment through the plugging of the crankcase vent valve, or simply because the oil is overdue for a change and has picked up condensation.

Likewise, pull the dipstick for the automatic-transmission fluid. Smell the fluid that clings to the stick. It should have a clean oil smell and should not smell burned. The fluid should have a reddish, translucent appearance; if it is black or muddy, it needs to be replaced right away. As for the general performance of the automatic transmission, it can be quickly and easily checked by accelerating lightly. Shifting should be clean and crisp through all gears, with no slipping. As with so many automotive preventive maintenance checks, this procedure is no different from normal driving — with the big difference that you do it while paying attention and *listening*.

The universal joints (or, on front-wheel-drive vehicles, the constant velocity joints) are another component that can sound the trouble alarm by means of erratic noises. A u-joint in its death throes makes a sound like birds chirping under the car at low speeds. As the car accelerates, so does the tempo of the birds' conversation, until around 30 mph it disappears altogether. Between 40 and 60 mph, you begin to notice a vibration under the floorboards. As the joint or joints deteriorate, the vibration will get more severe, and replacement is the only solution.

You may hear a whine from the differential during acceleration or deceleration, or while traveling at a steady speed. In the first two circumstances, the likelihood is that the differential's pinion bearings are getting ready to give out. If the sound occurs at a steady speed, the trouble probably lies with the main differential gears, or with the bearings at each side, called carrier bearings.

Bearing noise can also emanate from each of the four wheels, as each has a wheel bearing on which it turns. The sound to listen for is a steady grumbling, which can be confirmed as evidence of wheel-bearing problems by turning the car one way and the other. As you turn right, the right wheels will bear more weight and the noise will get more severe; meanwhile, the wheels on the left side may not grumble at all under their momentarily lightened load. Turn to the left, and the situation will reverse itself. Worn wheel bearings are a hazard and should be replaced without delay.

Improper wheel balance carries some characteristic symptoms, the most obvious of which is a shimmy at 40 mph and above. Along with the shimmy comes a tendency for the wheel to bounce erratically off the road. Needless to say, this type of wheel behavior adversely affects handling, braking, acceleration, and all-around safety. It also subjects the other front-end parts (notably ball joints) to more abuse in a hundred miles than might usually be experienced in several thousand.

So, pay attention to your car. Memorize its sounds, sights, and smells, both normal and abnormal, so that you can accurately convey them to your mechanic. If you can learn how to do this, he's much more likely to be able to make his diagnoses and repairs quickly and economically. Open your windows, turn off the air conditioner and the radio, and listen. Your car is talking to you. It's trying to tell you something.

Troubleshooting Chart

Troubleshooting automotive problems is best approached in terms of symptoms — sights, smells, sounds, movements, and experiences that depart from the norm. Some of these warning signs are relatively easy to pinpoint; smells, for example, can often be traced right to the source with little trouble. Certain sights and movements are also easy to interpret. Things aren't always so simple with the vast range of sounds — grinds, gratings, thumps, squeaks, and rattles that travel through the metal parts of the machine and in the process can get quite diffused. Sometimes it can take two people, one driving and one moving to different positions in the car, to isolate the area a noise is coming from.

Once the general area of an automotive problem is determined, one or more simple tests, outlined in the following chart, should be able to pinpoint the exact source. This is important both for the do-it-yourselfer and the motorist who intends to have a professional take care of the repairs. In the first case, it enables the home mechanic to take care of the problem quickly, effectively, and as inexpensively as possible. In the second case, proper prediagnosis helps the motorist to point the repairman in the right direction.

Within a big complicated modern engine lurk many dangers for the novice, who should beware of sticking a hand into a strange place in pursuit of trouble. Hands-on troubleshooting is best left to an expert.

All too often, a mechanic or service-order writer will hear a customer's complaint of a "grinding noise somewhere behind me," and consequently enter in the "Operation" column of the repair order, "Check noise in rear." What happens? The mechanic gets the car and may or may not road test it. He may open the trunk and find the jack and spare tire loose, secure them so that they don't rattle, and send the car on its way. When the customer picks up the car, he's back to square one.

The above may be an extreme example, and one that presupposes a mechanic with less commitment and enthusiasm than we might like to see. But the fact is, vague, imprecise descriptions of symptoms can often lead to vague, imprecise measures being taken to correct them. Be specific. The following chart is arranged according to sights, smells, sounds, movements, and experiences that spell trouble. Learn what these symptoms mean, and that trouble will be a lot easier to get rid of.

Changing a Flat

Flat tires aren't as common as they used to be, but that's no reason for not knowing how to deal with them. The first thing to do is to read the manual that came with the jack or the car — preferably before your tire goes flat. When trouble does come along, put the transmission in gear (park, for automatics), and set the emergency brake. Block both sides of the wheel diagonally opposite the one you are going to be working on — a couple of rocks will do.

Following the directions, start lifting the car with the jack, but don't relieve the weight from the wheel just yet. (By now, you should have taken the spare out of the trunk.) Next, loosen the lug nuts on the wheel with the flat. If the nuts stick, secure the lug wrench on each nut so that the handle is parallel with the ground, and stand on the wrench. Most lug nuts, by the way, are removed by turning them in a counterclockwise direction. There are some cars with left-handed threading on the nuts on the left side; these usually have an "L" stamped into the end of each lug and the nuts are removed by turning them clockwise.

Once all of the nuts have been loosened, start jacking the car again, and continue until the wheel is clear of the ground. Remove the nuts and the wheel. An easy way to get the spare wheel into position and onto the axle is to get down on one knee and insert the tip of your other foot beneath the wheel. Lift the wheel with your toes and guide it onto the lug nuts by hand. Anyone can do this.

Finally, put the nuts back on and hand-tighten them. Don't use the wrench to tighten nuts while the car is up on the jack. Lower the car, and then finish tightening with the wrench. As soon as possible, take the car into a garage and have the nuts torqued with a torque wrench.

Troubleshooting Guide

Sights

Symptom	Area	When
Blue smoke	Tail pipe	Starting or decelerating or when first stepping on gas after decelerating
Black smoke	Tail pipe	Running, trying to start
Gauge reads low or light flickers or comes on	Oil gauge or idiot light	Idling. When engine is warm
Gauge reads lower than at idle, or light flickers or comes on. Was off at lower speeds and at idle	Oil gauge or idiot light	Running at road speed with engine warm
Gauge reads low; heat from car's heater is weak, fuel economy usually suffers as well	Water-temp gauge runs too low or cold light will not go off	Running at idle or road speed when engine has been running at least five minutes
Gauge reads high or light* is on from the moment you turn the key to "on" * Note: *On all cars with idiot lights, it is normal for the hot light to come on when turning the ignition key to "start" position. This is to check the light bulb.*	Temp gauge runs too hot or hot light comes on	Running at idle or road speed

Sounds

Symptom	Area	When
Grinding noises under front of car at either front corner	Front of car—engine compartment	All the time the engine is running
Same as above	Same as above	Same as above
Same as above	At either front corner of car. Often can be felt in steering wheel	Only when car is moving, and relative to car's speed
Same as above	Same as above	Same as above

Cause	How to Pinpoint
Intake valve seals or piston rings	Engine uses more than one quart of oil in less than 700 miles.
Rich air-fuel mixture (carburetor)/plugged air filter/defective fuel injection/stuck choke	Have carburetor checked for sinking float. High float level indicates leaking needle valve or improper adjustments. Run car without air filter. If smoke is gone, replace air filter. Check position of choke plate. Hold it open if it is not already open. If smoke is gone, repair or adjust choke.
Low oil level/wrong viscosity oil for outside temperature/oil pump worn out or pressure-relief valve stuck/faulty signaling device (gauge or light)/major engine wear problems/oil diluted with unburned gas	Check dipstick for proper level. Change oil using proper grade or viscosity for outside temperature, as per owner's manual. Have a mechanic install his shop gauge to check actual oil pressure. If it is okay, problem is with gauge or light. If it checks low with his gauge, then there is a problem with oil pump, pressure-relief valve or engine.
Plugged or restricted oil filter/wrong viscosity oil for outside temperature/oil pickup screen in oil pan plugged/excessive sludge in bottom of oil pan	Change oil and filter using high-quality product and correct oil as per owner's manual. Remove oil pan and check pickup screen and pump, and clean sludge out of oil pan.
Thermostat will not close/stuck open/wrong thermostat in engine/no thermostat	Remove thermostat. If thermostat has been removed, install recommended one for car. (High temperature thermostat only). If there is a thermostat, test it in a pan of cold water on a stove. Thermostat should begin to open as water approaches 180°F. If it opens too soon, replace it. Test new thermostat before installing. It should open near temperature stamped on it. New products should be tested before installing them.
Faulty temperature gauge, sensor, or pinched or grounded wire in engine compartment	Turn key to "on" (run) but without starting engine. Engine should be cold. If temperature gauge is near hot position and/or hot light is on, open hood and locate temperature sensor. Remove wires. If gauge drops to cold or light goes off, sensor is faulty. If gauge remains up or light stays on, wire is grounded or pinched, or dash gauge unit is faulty.
Water pump	Open hood with engine running. Hold one end of a 3' or 4' section of old garden hose to your ear. Search engine compartment with other end. Hose will act as stethoscope.
Alternator	Same as above
Front wheel bearing	Wheel-bearing noise will most often disappear when weight is removed from a wheel. This means that if the noise lessens or goes away on a right turn, the offending bearing is the right front. The opposite is true for the left front.
Cupped worn tires (often mistaken for bad wheel bearing)	Same as above, but test should be preceded with a visual check of tires.

Troubleshooting Guide (cont.)

Sounds (cont.)

Symptom	Area	When
Grinding noises	At either rear corner of car	Only when the car is moving, and relative to car's speed
Same as above	Rear of engine compartment	Only when trying to start the engine
Same as above	Between driver and passenger on rear-wheel drive	All the time the engine is running or in a specific gear. When the car is moving.
Same as above	Same as above	Same as above
Grinding noise	Rear of car on rear-wheel drive; front of car on front-wheel drive	Reponsive to throttle position and road speed only when car is moving, and more pronounced at higher speeds
Same as above	Any or all four wheels	Could occur only when pressing the brake pedal to stop, or might happen when driving slowly
Backfire	Tail pipe	Coasting with foot off gas pedal
Backfire	Same as above	Trying to accelerate or trying to start engine
Heavy knocking noise that gets louder and goes faster as you increase speed	Engine	Driving at normal road speed
Exhaust sounds louder on acceleration	Under car	Engine running
Suspension rattle	Front or rear of car	Traveling over rough roads
Same as above	Same as above	Same as above
Body rattles	Any part of car	Same as above
Front tires will usually show excessive wear on the outer shoulders	Wheels/tires—front	Squeal when making a turn

Cause	How to Pinpoint
Rear wheel bearings	Same as above
Starter	Simple. Try to start engine. Noises? Remove starter for inspection.
Transmission (standard)	Drive car in each gear, making note of changes in noise. If present only in some gears and not others, noise is in the transmission. Transmission noises will almost always disappear when coasting in neutral. If a transmission noise occurs when the engine is running and car is not moving, it will disappear when the clutch is depressed.
Transmission (automatic)	Most automatic-transmission noises are about the same as water-pump and alternator noises. They can be pinpointed with the homemade stethoscope.
Differential—rear axle	On a level road, bring car to a legal speed. Close window and turn off all accessories. Usually a rear-end noise will occur either on acceleration or deceleration. It will disappear or change pitch when holding a steady speed or changing throttle setting.
Brakes	It is best heard with car windows open and head or ear (if ear is that big) partially out open window. Bring car to normal stop from legal road speed. Vary pressure on brake pedal; if noise changes, brakes are suspect. If noise occurs at slow speed without applying brake pedal pressure, apply brakes normally while moving. If noise disappears or changes, brakes are suspect.
Exhaust emission component called decel valve	Only makes noise when coasting or when shifting gears on manual transmission car.
Ignition timing/leaking exhaust valve/sparkplug wires crossed/ cracked or wet distributor cap	Check all ignition components and replace as needed. If ignition is okay, take compression test of engine.
Major parts of engine coming apart	It's too late to check the oil—you've done it this time. Shut it down and call a tow truck.
Hole in front exhaust pipe or muffler	Raise car on lift and inspect exhaust system.
Loose shocks, worn shock bushings	Raise car on lift that keeps the weight of the car on the wheels. Grab and shake shock. Worn bushings or loose mounts will be evident. Bounce car up and down and listen.
Loose or worn suspension pivot points	Refer to car maker's manual for procedure. The type of suspension you have will determine the testing procedure.
Loose parts	This is usually a two-person project: one driving and one listening and holding parts until rattle is found.
Front-end alignment/low tire pressure/weak shocks/going too fast around corners	Align front end/inflate tires to proper pressure/test shocks and replace as needed/slow down.

Troubleshooting Guide (cont.)

Sounds (cont.)

Symptom	Area	When
Gets louder the faster you drive. Front tires are hot and could get hot enough to smoke	Same as above	Tires squeal when going straight ahead
Squeal or grind when applying brake	Wheels or tire area	Only when car is moving and brakes are applied. Gets louder the faster the car is going

Smells

Symptom	Area	When
Exhaust smell in car	In car	Engine running
Accompanied by smoke, smells like asbestos (that's what it is) cooking	Any or all four wheels	Driving or just after stopping
Same as above, but only cars with manual transmissions	From under the middle of the car	Same as above
Hot, oily, burning smell. Smoke might also be present	From under hood	Engine warm
Same as above	From under car	Same as above
Rotten-egg odor	Tail pipe	Engine running
Gasoline smell	Inside car	All the time

Movements

Symptom	Area	When
Car hits bottom. Common term "bottoming" refers to suspension reaching end of its travel	Under car	Going over bumps
Car floats or rocks up and down after going over bumps	General	After bumps while riding along
Car pulls right or left	Brakes	Applying brakes

Cause	How to Pinpoint
Bent steering linkage/front-end alignment/worn steering and/or suspension components	Get car to shop right away, preferably on a tow truck with front wheels off ground.
Worn brake shoes or pads/rotors or drums need resurfacing	Remove wheels for visual inspection. Replace parts as needed.

Cause	How to Pinpoint
Exhaust leak in tail pipe	Tail-pipe exhaust leaks do not necessarily cause a noise like a muffler or front exhaust pipe. To check an exhaust system for leaks, start engine and let idle. Using a rag, cover end of tail pipe to restrict exhaust flow. If system is solid, you will not be able to hold exhaust back.
Hard braking or dragging brakes	Look and sniff.
Slipping or riding the clutch	Look and sniff.
Oil leaking on hot engine parts	Open hood and visually check for oil leaks on outside of engine.
Transmission-fluid leak hitting hot exhaust components.	There is no way to pinpoint this.
Excessive fuel reaching catalytic converter due to faulty ignition, carburetion, or mechanical problems	With engine running and transmission in neutral or park and emergency brake applied, walk to back of car and sniff.
Leak in fuel line	Shut off engine and open hood. Inspect visually. If there are no signs of a leak, call a mechanic.

Cause	How to Pinpoint
Shocks or springs	Check shocks as previously described. Replace if indicated. If bottoming still occurs, replace springs. If you are carrying heavy loads, consider overload springs.
Bad shocks	Bounce each end of car and let go. The car should stop bouncing after one more complete up and down motion. If it continues, replace shocks. Check shocks for evidence of hydraulic fluid leaking. Replace if leaks found.
Brake fluid on brake lining/grease on lining/unbalanced lining/rotors or drums requiring turning (machining)/tire pressure uneven	Remove wheels (all four) for visual inspection, check tire pressure.

Troubleshooting Guide (cont.)

Movements (cont.)

Symptom	Area	When
Car pulls to the right or left, when you let go of the wheel	Steering	Driving down any straight, level road

Experiences

Symptom	Area	When
Engine won't start. No sound when turning key or just click-click	Engine	Engine will not turn over when key is turned
Same as above	Same as above	Same as above
Engine won't start. Starter sounds normal	Same as above	Engine turns over normally but will not start
Same as above	Same as above	Same as above
Engine starts and stalls when transmission shifted to reverse or drive. Restarts easily	Same as above	Starting cold
Same as above, but difficult to restart and continues to stall. Also black smoke noted out of tail pipe	Same as above	Same as above
Hesitates and/or stalls on acceleration	Same as above	All the time, hot or cold
Dies when running at road speed or climbing hills, but when speed or load drops, engine runs fine	Same as above	Anytime, hot or cold
Same as above	Same as above	Same as above

Cause	How to Pinpoint
Tires/front-end alignment/dragging brakes/defective steering gear/tire pressure uneven	Some radial tires tend to lead (pull to one side). A good front-end mechanic, when diagnosing this problem, will swap the two front tires and road test again. If the pull disappears or goes the other way, the tires are at fault. Tires should be the same size, and tread pattern should be the same. Align front end. In a front-end alignment procedure, a good front-end man will check worn suspension parts, shocks, dragging brakes, and steering components before aligning car.

Cause	How to Pinpoint
Dead battery	Car starts normally when boosters are used.
Loose or dirty battery cables	Battery-to-battery cable connection is hot to the touch after trying to start car.
Ignition system malfunction	Remove one spark plug wire. Insert a spark plug in wire and ground spark plug shell to engine with a jumper wire. Open gap on plug. Have someone turn engine over while watching for spark to jump plug gap. Good blue spark, ignition system okay. Yellow, orange, or no spark, ignition system needs work.
Fuel system	With ignition off, engine stopped, remove air filter and check position of choke plate. On a cold engine, it should be closed. On a warm engine, it should be open. If not, repair. If choke is okay, hold in open position. Using flashlight, look down into throttle carburetor throat. Open throttle suddenly and watch for one or more solid streams of gasoline injected into carburetor throat. If not present, problem could be carburetor or fuel-delivery system.
Carburetor, automatic choke, fuel-injection cold-start injector or temp sensor	Refer to shop manual for particular car. Adjust or replace choke, carburetor, or fuel-injection components as needed.
Automatic choke, choke vacuum diaphragm, leaking cold-start injector	Check choke adjustment, test vacuum diaphragm, or test cold-start injector as per shop manual.
Accelerator pump in carburetor	With engine turned off, remove air filter. Hold choke open. Aim flashlight (not a match, please) down into the throat of carburetor. Open throttle wide and you should see a stream of gas being sprayed into carburetor bore (one for single-barrel carburetor, two for 2- and 4-barrel carburetors.) If no gas is being sprayed, accelerator pump or passageways need attention.
Fuel filter plugged	Replace filter
Fuel pump defective or worn out	Check fuel-pump pressure, volume, and vacuum as per shop manual.

Troubleshooting Guide (cont.)

Experiences (cont.)

Symptom	Area	When
Engine skips and runs rough at high speeds or accelerating	Same as above	Same as above
Dies when running at road speed and will not restart	Same as above	Same as above
Rear of car hanging too low	Rear of car	Car sitting on level ground
One side or corner of car lower than the rest	Side or corner of car	Car sitting on level ground

Cause	How to Pinpoint
Spark plugs, plug wires, distributor cap, rotor, or ignition coil	Perform tuneup if indicated by mileage since last one (more than 10,000 miles), replacing spark plugs. Check wires with ohmmeter and visually inspect distributor cap and rotor. Test coil as per manual.
Fuel or ignition system	If starter will turn engine over, the engine is not seized. Battery and electrical system are also probably okay. Check fuel gauge. If near E, *get gas*. To check fuel system, remove air-filter top. Hold choke open. Aim flashlight into carburetor bore. Open throttle wide. You should see one or two streams of fuel being sprayed into carburetor bore. If so, the fuel system should start the car. If not, fuel system defective. Remove a wire from a spark plug and put the end near a ground (½″ away). Have someone turn engine over while watching for a spark. A blue spark ½″ long is okay. A yellow or orange spark is a weak spark. If spark is weak or if there is no spark at all, the ignition system is malfunctioning. If ignition system and fuel system are okay, there could be engine problems. Call a tow truck.
Weak rear springs (not shocks)/too much junk in the trunk/rear tires smaller than front	Check tire size on all four tires. Unless you drive a 1984 Corvette, they should all be the same and have about the same tread. Go on a scavenger hunt in the trunk and keep only the really neat stuff, like the spare and jack and a legitimate emergency kit. If the back is still a pavement scraper, replace rear springs.
Wrong size tire on that wheel/ weak or broken spring or springs	Check tire sizes. If not the same, make correction as needed. If still low, replace spring. *Note:* Springs should be replaced in pairs; i.e., both fronts or both rears.

All the Trimmings: A Guide to Accessories

One of the nicer things — and yet one of the more challenging and confusing — about buying a new car is the vast number of accessory options available. We can generally assign these options to either of two categories — those installed at the factory and those you can add on yourself at or after the time of purchase — and that's the way we'll look at them in this chapter. First, though, we should make a point of remembering that any and all automotive accessories serve one basic purpose: to help a car fit the personality, needs, and driving style of its owner. If a car doesn't fit those requirements, the owner will never really be happy with it and will probably come to think of it as a lemon no matter how well it works.

Even when your mind is made up as to the basic model you want, you shouldn't walk into the showroom without some firm ideas as to what you desire in the way of options. The reason? Car salesmen love to load up a car with accessory options, since that is where a good percentage of their profit lies. A clever salesman may very well pare the base price of a car down to the point where you're practically buying it at cost, and then start selling you options that will bring the price way back up and guarantee a good margin for himself and the agency. It can happen that the list cost of a car's accessories will approach two-thirds of its original base price, particularly if it started as a relatively inexpensive model and a lot of options were available. If you walk into the showroom without your accessory shopping list in order, you leave yourself at the mercy of the hard sell and may wind up with not so much of a "deal" after all.

With this precaution in mind, let's look at some of the more popular accessories and basic equipment options, beginning with the engine and drive train.

Cruising

Cruise control is probably the most useful of all accessory items for anyone who does a lot of long-distance driving. The nicest thing about it is that it takes all of the throttle-setting decisions away from the driver and eliminates any tendency to pump the gas pedal, a practice that wastes fuel. Cruise control assures a steady throttle position, improving fuel economy and assuring a steady ride. Perhaps best of all, it relieves driver fatigue.

Regardless of the setting chosen, cruise control automatically disconnects when you hit the brake. Most newer units have a resume feature, though, which enables you to bring the car back up to the pre-set speed with the touch of a single button.

Cruise control can either be factory installed or chosen as an after-market option. If you're looking at a car on the lot that does not come with factory cruise control, the dealer should be able to install it for you for under $200. It shouldn't be necessary, though, if 90 percent or more of your driving is around town.

Engine Options

With the exception of a few small cars in which only one engine is available, each model is offered with a base engine that can be upgraded at the buyer's discretion. This engine is nearly always the most fuel-efficient power plant compatible with the car, because that is how manufacturers meet the fleet average miles-per-gallon requirement mandated by the federal government. It can generally be assumed, then, that your basic engine will almost always be the most efficient, and probably the most lackluster in terms of performance. If you are going to be doing any serious amount of highway driving, and are concerned about having the acceleration capability for safe passing and entry-ramp merging, it's a good idea to go to the next-higher-performance engine on the list of available options. (One exception is the General Motors J-cars, in which the 1.8 liter basic four-cylinder engine is superior to the optional 2.0 liter model.)

At the other end of the spectrum of available engines you will find the larger-displacement, high-performance engines. Nowadays we are back in the world of high performance, having left it at the end of the sixties' "muscle car" era because of rising fuel costs and the advent of emissions controls. What happened is that engineers learned how to use things like electronic fuel injection, electronic spark timing, and computer controls to coax impressive performance out of engines not nearly as large and a good deal more efficient than those that gave the muscle era its name. So, you've got a choice: you can select your engine for fuel economy, average highway driving, or high performance.

Transmissions

The basic choice here is between automatic and standard transmission, although of course the larger domestic cars are all equipped with automatics and generally cannot be purchased with standard.

Within the realm of standard or "stick" shift, there are two further options: four speeds or five.

Be careful when making your choice between four-speed and five-speed manual transmissions. Unless you are a sophisticated driver, you may not notice any appreciable difference except that you will be doing a bit more shifting. As far as fuel efficiency goes, most manufacturers are making the top gear in a four-speed gearbox the same highway cruising gear (i.e., it has the same ratio) as fifth gear in a five-speed setup. Official test figures may show a difference in gasoline consumption of one-half or one mile per gallon between the two options at highway speeds, but in practical, everyday driving, even this small difference will probably not show up. However, if you are driving with an eye toward performance and don't mind shifting, you'll probably find a five-speed to be a lot of fun. They usually have a closer gear ratio (less difference in engine speed between each gear) for a smoother power curve over the entire operating range, which translates into greater involvement and more of a sports car feel.

Most automatic transmissions available today are of the four-speed overdrive variety with lock-up torque converter and are simply not the smooth-as-silk automatics of yore. For the reasons stated in chapter 6, the lock-up converter causes the new transmissions to operate a bit more roughly, as it engages and disengages in response to situations such as grades or other heavy loads. This syndrome is most noticeable with smaller engines, and when a car has a full complement of passengers.

Selecting the Rear-End Ratio

The average driver is often confused when presented with a choice of rear axle gear ratios. But making the selection is really quite simple if you remember one important rule of thumb: the lower the gear ratio, the slower the car will be in pulling away from a standing start, the more efficiently it will cruise along the highway, and the better the overall fuel economy it will have. Conversely, the higher the gear ratio, the quicker the car will jump away from the traffic light, and the lower the highway gas mileage will be. The high gear ratio is something you'll want if you plan to be towing a trailer, since it will enable you to pull off from a start without balking and crawling.

Choices in Suspension Packages

Towing is also a consideration in choosing a suspension package. If you plan to tow, look for an option package that includes trailer-towing suspension. First, though, make sure such a package is available with the car you plan to buy. The Pontiac Division of the General Motors Corporation has recently issued a statement recommending that *none* of its cars be used for towing trailers. Developments such as this reflect the fact that fuel economy and emissions standards, as mandated by the government, rule automotive engineering today. Regardless of how we may feel about this, it is a reality we will have to live with.

Other suspension options range from soft to firm. The Jeep Wagoneer offers a "soft ride" option, which amounts to a mushier ride than the one you get with the standard suspension. At the other extreme are the so-called firm-ride, special-handling, or "rally-tuned suspension" packages. These packages give the automobile greater stability at highway speed, as well as on narrow back roads and corners. In any event, try to avoid a car with wallowing, wandering suspension, which is dangerous at any speed.

Some manufacturers offer a load-carrying package, which includes air shock absorbers with automatic leveling controls on the rear and sometimes on all four wheels. These automatically compensate for the presence or absence of heavy passenger or cargo loads, so that the headlights stay aimed correctly and the car

doesn't squat at its tail. The system runs off a compressor under the hood (operated either via engine vacuum or electricity) and a central microprocessor — or, in the new Lincoln Continental Mark VII, four separate microprocessors connected through a main computer and compressor. With its four air shocks, the Lincoln can not only vary its load-carrying capability, but also tailor the suspension to the type of road surface being driven upon.

Tire and Wheel Combinations

Some suspension packages also include differences in tire and wheel combinations. Like the basic engines, the standard-equipment tires on new cars are usually chosen for their low rolling resistance and beneficial effects on gas mileage. These are narrower tires with limited handling capability and skid resistance, and you may wish to upgrade them in order to improve responsiveness in these areas. If you opt for the rally-tuned suspension, this will usually be done automatically.

An improved suspension package will usually include better wheels as well. Wheels such as the new cast-aluminum-alloy ones are usually lighter than the standard variety, and lightness is important. The lighter the wheel-tire-brake combination, the better the car rides. This is because the wheel assembly constitutes *unsprung* weight, meaning that it lies between the road and the springs, and the lighter the wheel the less it will bounce. Also, the light wheels will usually accept a tire with a more aggressive tread, such as the Michelin TRX. (Of course, you'll have to continue buying the high-performance tires that fit your high-performance wheels.)

As for hubcaps, they're your choice. Remember, though, that the cast-alloy wheels are their own decoration and seldom have extraneous hubcaps. This eliminates the problem of hubcap theft. Of course, thieves can take your whole wheel, but they would have done that anyway, hubcap and all.

Heavy-Duty Cooling Systems

Why would you want a heavy-duty radiator? There are a number of possible reasons. One is sustained driving in hot weather, either over the road or in heavy city traffic. Another is towing a trailer. Still another, and perhaps the most important of all, is to complement an air-conditioning system. If the heavy-duty cooling package isn't part of the air-conditioning deal, specify it separately. Otherwise, you may overheat the engine under heavy summer a.c. loads.

Heavy-Duty Battery and Alternator

This is a handy option if you live in a cold climate. It gives you additional cold cranking power for more reliable starting on frigid winter mornings. The higher-output alternator puts more energy back into the battery when the car is running — a good thing to have when you're stuck in traffic with the lights, radio, and heater on. Heavy air-conditioning loads in warm climates also make this an attractive option.

Air Conditioning

It's easy to write off air conditioning as a warm-climate option, or to look at it as a luxury that gets in the way of good gas mileage. But actually, it's useful throughout the country and doesn't have to be that much of a drain on mileage. A factory air conditioner can be operated to the driver's and passengers' advantage almost twelve months a year. This is because it *dehumidifies* as well as cools and incorporates the heating apparatus as well. When temperatures are just above freezing and the humidity is high, you can use the air conditioner to both warm and dehumidify the car, so you stay more comfortable and the windows stay clear of fog. If it's raining and you've already gotten wet, the air conditioner's dehumidification feature will even dry you and your clothes.

In a sense, air conditioning can even be a safety feature. During a long, hot-weather trip, the endless drone of road noise that pours into the car when you open the window can actually cause fatigue. With the air conditioner on and the windows rolled up, not only heat but noise is locked out.

Now for that question of air conditioning and gas mileage. Cars today are designed aerodynamically, to slip through the air as effortlessly as possible while using a minimum of fuel. When you open the windows, you upset the car's built-in

Stormy Weather

Fashions change, and so do auto accessories. Why, in 1905 no self-respecting motorist would be caught dead without his duster, a light cotton coat (much like a shop coat) to cover and protect his fancy frock coat, along with his goggles, cap, and huge-cuffed driving gloves.

By the mid-twenties these accessories were things of the past, as cars now had windshields and some form of a top. But a new fashion emerged: the raccoon coat. The heater had not been invented and the tops and windows of the cars then fit loosely. With cars finally being driven year round, the 'coon coat did the job of keeping Jazz Age motorists and their passengers warm.

Cold-weather driving prompted an accessory to be installed even in those cars equipped with heaters. This was the robe rail, a place to hang your lap robe on the back of the front seat. This trend continued until the current crop of front and rear heater and air-conditioning systems were adopted in the sixties.

aerodynamics. If the air conditioner is working properly and you don't have it set too cold, the load it places on the engine at highway speeds is often actually less than the extra load that would be imposed by opening the windows and defeating the aerodynamic design.

Selecting an air-conditioning package usually involves making a choice between automatic temperature control and conventional controls. Most people will find the manual controls sufficient, although the automatic setup is tempting: it lets you set the temperature you want and leave it all year, while taking care of dehumidification at the same time (Note: you might wish to consider air conditioning as an add-on or "after market" accessory.)

No one has a choice any longer regarding heaters. As recently as the 1960s, Ford made some cars for the Florida market with no heaters, but now they are standard equipment on all automobiles made in the United States.

Cold-Climate Engine Warmup Options

In cold climates, most manufacturers offer an engine warming kit. This option, which should be thought of as an absolute necessity with diesel engines, plugs into a wall outlet and keeps the engine coolant warm overnight. This in turn keeps the oil from thickening into molasses, keeps the combustion chambers warm, and makes the car a lot easier to start in the morning.

Seating Options

Now let's look into the passenger compartment and see what we have available in the way of seats. The first option evident to most buyers is bucket seats, as opposed to bench seating. Bucket seats have become virtually universal, and by now are even standard equipment in many

Bucket seats like these offer comfort and security — if properly designed — and give lateral support on turns to driver and passenger. This 1984 model sports an extra luxury feature — stereo speakers in each headrest.

cars. They are comfortable, secure seats — that is, if they are designed properly and are fully adjustable over a range of back positions and distances from the wheel. Bucket seats, unlike bench seats, offer lateral support to driver and front-seat passenger, especially when rounding bends. Bench seats are definitely becoming a thing of the past, but if you are used to them after years of driving, don't be afraid to specify them. It's your car, after all, and it should be built to fit you.

Power-adjustable seats are strictly a matter of personal choice. They're fun to have — at least for some buyers — but they border on belonging to the same class as windshield wipers on your sunglasses. Remember that many of the most expensive and luxurious European cars don't have power seats. They aren't found on Mercedes, for instance, until you get up into the $50,000 380 series. The fact is that manual seats just aren't that hard to adjust.

What about power windows? At first glance, they seem almost as frivolous as power seats. But there is an instance in which power windows may actually act as a safety feature. Picture yourself leaving a toll booth, wallet in hand. It's summer, and you have the air conditioner on — or it's the dead of winter, with the heater going — and you're trying to shift gears and put your money away at the same time. If you feel as if you need another hand, you'll understand why power windows might be a godsend.

The three selections in seat coverings are cloth, vinyl, and leather. There was a time when cloth was the standard and vinyl was the option. But cloth seats are making a comeback, thanks to new fabrics that resist stains and wash clean without leaving water marks. Cloth seats are warmer in the winter and cooler in the summer; you don't stick to them when they're hot, or slide around in them. Last but not least, they simply look nice.

If you have animals and/or small children, though, it may be best to stay with vinyl. If you have neither pets nor kids but do have extra cash, leather may be for you. But make sure there is *plenty* of extra cash: a leather interior can add $3,000, $4,000, or even $5,000 to the cost of a car, if it is offered at all.

Floor Protection

Almost all cars today come with carpeting, rather than vinyl, as a standard floor covering. All car manufacturers, however, offer optional kick mats, or carpet inserts, as additional floor protection. These are always a good idea, since they keep carpets from wearing out. When you buy them, go with the ones sold by the manufacturer, not the discount store down the road. The mats made to fit your car will match the color exactly, while the cut-rate item will neither match nor fit properly and will make your new car look five years old. If they bunch up around the pedals, they may even be dangerous.

Another problem with the all-vinyl mats sold separately is that they do not breathe. Water trapped between the carpet and the mat may rot the carpet fabric, leaving you worse off than if you had had no mats at all. Mats made of cocoa fiber are good, since they absorb moisture and dirt and let the carpeting breathe. They are thick, though, so it's a good idea to "test drive" these mats before you buy to make sure you are comfortable with the way they feel.

Lighting Options

Auto manufacturers offer something called a "light group" for most of the models they sell. This is a simple way of putting all of the courtesy lights — glove compartment, trunk, ashtray, under hood, etc. — in one group and selling them for one price. Usually, this one price is lower than what you'd pay to have each of these lights installed individually, and it saves the manufacturer the trouble of having to cater to dozens of different, specially ordered combinations.

Tinted Glass

Some car manufacturers have made tinted glass standard on all of their models; others include it as standard equipment only on cars with air conditioning. Especially in areas where the sun is strong, tinted glass does make the inside of the car cooler and cuts down on air-conditioning loads. That means better gas mileage. On some cars, particularly station wagons and vans, heavily tinted glass is making an appearance. This is a smoky, almost one-way glass. Aside from questions about its visibility value for the driver, though, it cannot be heartily recommended because of the efforts of many police departments to have it made illegal. The reason is simple: when a policeman approaches a stopped car or van, he very understandably likes to be able to see what's going on inside. The same prohibitions would of course apply to sheet-plastic tinting affixed to the glass.

The black metal or plastic louvres seen on the rear windows of some fastbacks and hatchbacks are not just ornamentation. These, too, can make the inside of the car cooler — and cut air-conditioning loads — by keeping out direct sunlight.

Windshield Wipers

Windshield wipers and washers are now standard on all cars. Some makers offer the "intermittent wiper" option in which there is a setting below normal wiper operation at which the wiper blades make a sweep across the windshield every eight seconds or so. This is good when there is a fine mist or light drizzle in the air, since not enough water would gather on the windshield under those conditions to allow the blades to become sufficiently lubricated and prevent them from streaking and chattering along their course. Sometimes, you'll even have a choice between pre-set and adjustable intervals between strokes. All in all, intermittent wipers are a boon to drivers who spend a lot of time on the highway.

Paint and Trim

Paint and trim options are purely a matter of the buyer's personal taste. This category of options includes the popular vinyl roofs, about which one word of caution is in order: water tends to hide under the vinyl and can cause rusting around the window areas of the car.

It may be hard to imagine how the color of a car could affect interior comfort and fuel economy, but the fact is that lighter-colored automobiles reflect more heat, and thus keep cooler on the inside in hot climates. If the car has air conditioning, this of course means a lighter a.c. load, with the resulting slight improvements in gas mileage.

If you live in the nation's "rust belt" — places where road salt and slush keep up a five-month-a-year attack on your car — rustproofing is absolutely essential. This will coat and protect unseen surfaces. The parts of the car that show should also be protected, with a paint sealer that will minimize the effects of weather and dirt and keep the car looking good until resale time.

Side Moldings

Another way to preserve the value and appearance of your car is to specify the rubberized moldings that can be installed along the doors and side panels of the car. (The moldings can usually be added later, if they were not standard or if you neglected to order them.) These serve as the point of contact for the other car doors that are inevitably opened thoughtlessly in parking lots and other tight spots, and keep your doors and fenders from being covered with dents and dings. This is a plus at trade-in time, since even a well-kept engine cannot make up for a body that looks like it has been gone over with a ball-peen hammer.

Extra bumper guards were once recommended for the same reason as the side moldings — to protect chrome and paint from parking abuses. But the guards are not compatible with the plastic fascia used in lieu of bumpers on many new cars, nor are they necessary any longer — the impact-absorbing plastic is more than capable of soaking up minor punishment.

Sun or Moon Roofs

Sun roofs or moon roofs — whatever the manufacturer calls them, are fun to have. But if you don't like the glare of the sun, don't get a glass roof insert, because most of them don't have opaque cover panels. This means the sun will always be there, whether you want it or not. If this annoys you, so might the staccato glare of passing overhead streetlamps when you're driving down a city street. On cars with air conditioning, these roofs become a less desirable option, since you wouldn't want one open when the a.c. is on, and a glass panel

The sun/moon roof shown here can be installed after a car has been manufactured. Most, however, can only be installed in the factory, and can't be removed if sun, moon or streetlight glare become a liability.

admitting solar glare is only going to put more of a strain on the system.

The Decline of the Full-Size Spare

If it is at all possible, specify a full-size spare tire. These have been disappearing of late as standard equipment, and in their place we are finding the little emergency or "space-saver" spares. These are good for about fifty miles of driving, at speeds that should not exceed forty or fifty miles an hour. This may not be much help if you get a flat on a weekend in the middle of nowhere and have to wait until Monday morning to have your regular tire fixed or buy a new one. Also, if you specify the big, conventional spare, you can use it as part of your tire rotation, and get some wear out of it in return for the money it cost.

"After Market" Accessories

All of the accessories you want on your car might not be available as factory-installed equipment. Or, you may decide after tak-

ing delivery that there are items worth adding that you overlooked when placing your order. These are called the "after market" accessories, and their numbers probably run into the hundreds. In the next few pages, we'll take a look at a few of the more popular items.

Air Conditioning

There was a time, not so long ago, when add-on air conditioning had a pretty dismal reputation. Today, however, there are after-market units that are as good as or better than much of the factory air. Many of them can take in outside air and can even mix it with heated air. To look at the best of them, you'd never know they weren't factory-installed.

When adding an air conditioner to a new car, though, you should give some serious thought to the warranty. Ideally, the warranty on the add-on unit would have the same duration as that which applies to the car itself, but this is not always the case. Still, there are times when even a less favorable warranty is worth overlooking, such as when you are offered a good deal on an as-is, off-the-lot new car without air and have the option of installing a unit yourself. Think it over; after-market air conditioning can be a sensible alternative.

Sound Systems

The days when a radio was a radio are long gone. Now, we have everything from the simplest AM sets to top-of-the-line systems like the Delco-Bose, available on Cadillacs and other GM premium models and carefully balanced to custom-fit each car. There is a vast spectrum in between, which includes not only the radio receivers and speakers themselves but also an assortment of power amplifiers, linear boosters, and graphic equalizers designed to cut distortion, improve fidelity, and — in the case of the equalizers — allow you to accentuate or mute different ranges within the sound spectrum at will.

Recommending sound systems is a subjective business, and one that could easily fill a book of its own. There are, however, a few broad generalizations we might make. Most aficionados of good auto sound agree that separate bass and treble controls are usually a sign of a unit's superiority over models featuring a single bass-treble knob. Also, electronic tuning — with a digital display of the station number in tune — is more precise and easier to operate while driving than the traditional "slide rule" tuning mechanism.

If you're investing in high-quality sound reproduction, a four-way speaker system makes good sense. Try installing two smaller speakers in front, for response in the higher-frequency ranges, and two larger speakers in the rear for accurate bass rendition.

A tape player is a good idea for anyone who does a lot of long-distance driving, for the simple reason that FM stations tend to fade once you get forty miles or so away from the transmitter. Playing your own music will save you the trouble of fussing with the dial. Both 8-track cartridges and cassettes are available, although cassettes are beginning to eclipse the older cartridge systems and are much easier to store.

One further thing to remember: if you plan to install your own sound system, and wish the factory to subtract the standard-equipment radio that comes with the car you're ordering, make sure the dealer gives you appropriate credit.

Seat Covers

Modern car upholstery is sturdy and attractive, and as we noted earlier it is available in a wide variety of fabrics, vinyl, and leather. You're paying for it, so you may as well enjoy it. Why cover new car upholstery with add-on seat covers? It's far better to wait until the car gets old and the seats really need new covers. You aren't doing yourself any favors by concealing the factory upholstery so that it stays new and unused while the rest of the car ages; it won't help the resale value, since the car's true condition will be obvious to a prospective buyer from the shape the exterior is in.

If your original seats have begun to show their age, good seat covers can of course improve their appearance. But shop around — sometimes it's possible to have the driver's seat rebuilt and re-upholstered (after all, that's the seat that shows the wear) for no more money than a full set of covers would cost.

Tools and Safety Items

A useful automobile tool kit might contain a crescent wrench, vise grip and regular pliers, and Phillips and regular screwdrivers. In addition, it's a good idea to carry spare quart cans of engine oil and transmission fluid, and a gallon each of anti-freeze-water mix and windshield washer fluid. Round out the kit with a good flashlight, a funnel, a collapsible bucket, a rag, and pair of panty hose. Panty hose? Yes, to use as an emergency fan belt. Tie them tight around the pulleys and away you go — slowly, of course — to the nearest service station to have a new belt installed. Thorough-minded drivers might also wish to throw in a nylon tow strap, a pair of battery booster cables, and a four-way lug wrench.

Every car should have a small first-aid kit, including bandages, ointments, and disinfectants. You can buy kits of varying sizes at most auto-supply shops, or put one together yourself using a biscuit tin or Tupperware container. A blanket is another nice thing to have on board. Aside from its obvious purpose during the winter, it will come in handy year round should you have to get down on the ground to make repairs.

There's no reason to travel without a fire extinguisher. They're compact, inexpensive, and easy to use. But remember: whether it's your car or someone else's, don't try to play hero by attempting to put out a major fire with a hand-held extinguisher. *Get the passengers out of danger first;* once they are safe, let the car burn. It's insured. Use the fire extinguisher only on small, localized, easily controllable fires.

Alarms and Locks

Automobile security devices run the gamut from add-on equipment designed to slow down a thief, to electronic wizardry that makes theft all but impossible without a tow truck. The Chapman Lock secures all means of entrance into the car, including the hood, as well as shutting off the electrical system. The driver deactivates the system and prevents an alarm from sounding by inserting his key in a lock and turning a T-handle, both inside the car, within a set period after opening the door. Other locks require the insertion of a key in an outside receptacle *before* the doors are opened.

Even more foolproof are the new coded, computerized devices with control centers hidden inside the car, either under the dash, under the seat, or inside the glove compartment. These require the operator to punch in a pre-set code before starting the car. If the wrong code is entered, or the procedure takes too long, the car fails to start and a deafening alarm goes off. A useful bonus feature of these systems is that they double as sobriety testers — if you have had one too many, you aren't likely to get the code punched in, in time to drive away.

Less elaborate equipment designed to make a thief's work more difficult includes the Crook-lock, an iron bar with crooked ends, which anchors the steering wheel to the brake pedal; and the locked-steering-wheel cuff, which makes it impossible to get at the ignition switch. Also, there are smooth-topped door buttons designed to thwart coat hangers, and bolt-on steel plates that cover trunk locks. As for the notorious Slim Jim, which thieves slide between door and window to pop door locks, car makers are now installing hidden baffles that make the devices difficult or impossible to use.

Special Headlights and Driving Lights

Anyone who does much nighttime driving should invest in a set of halogen quartz headlights and auxiliary fog lights. Replacement halogen quartz lamps can be purchased for the headlight sockets in any car; they're more expensive, but they're worth the money when it comes to slicing through the darkness on back roads. There's no truth to the story that a pair of oncoming quartz lights will endanger a driver in the opposite lane — *if* they are properly aimed. Accurate headlight alignment is a must if you are going to use these lights.

Fog lights, or driving lights as they are sometimes called, should also be of the halogen quartz type. Shop carefully for these lights — some of the "bargain" sets aren't bargains at all, since all they contain are ordinary dome lights. You may as well mount two candles on the bumper as drive with these. Actually, non-halogen fog lights are dangerous, since they may give you a false sense of confidence.

Mudflaps

Many drivers are upset — and rightly so — by the "sandblasting" effect of sand, salt, and gravel thrown up onto front and rear fenders by the wheels. A set of small mudflaps is the traditional approach to this problem, and it still works well. However, some auto manufacturers are offering a clear plastic film to protect the paint in these areas; this film is also available as an after-market accessory. Results with this product to date have been largely satisfactory.

Power Antennas

Unlike their earlier counterparts, today's power antennas are mostly reliable devices. If you don't order one as factory-installed equipment, you can probably add a unit for between $30 and $80. They retract and extend automatically with the operation of the ignition. Power antennas might almost be considered a necessity in cities, where young thugs take delight in snapping antennas off cars.

Luggage Racks

As cars get smaller, so do their trunks, and luggage racks begin to make more and more sense to the long-distance traveler. The main precaution here is to make sure of the load capacity of the rack you buy. A flimsy little rack will collapse under the weight of heavy luggage, an experience that will be all the more unpleasant when you are hundreds of miles from home.

Shop wisely for accessories, and equip your car to suit your practical needs and reasonable esthetic preferences. If you do, chances are that resale value will be improved as well. Just don't overdo it. The "hillbilly hotrod" has a limited resale market, and foxtails went out in the fifties.

Dressing It Up

When shopping for a new car or upgrading the old bus, look for accessories that will increase the value of the car as well as make it more enjoyable to own and drive.

Vinyl roofs and similar dress-up gadgets may improve the looks and thereby make you feel better about the car, but do little else. Cruise control, the device that keeps your car's speed at a predetermined setting, could save money on gas for the over-the-road driver as well as help stave off some speeding tickets. On the other hand, for the driver who seldom ventures out on the highway, cruise control could be a gigantic waste of money.

Choose the add-ons for your car with an eye to the kind of driving you do and the resale value of your car.

Buying and Selling to Your Best Advantage

Buying a new car is a landmark occasion in anyone's life, especially the first time around. There's something about picking out an automobile — even a used one — that invites emotion to take over from cool reason. But exciting as it may be, buying a car just because it turns you on can be a sure prescription for trouble. Even given the need for some minor compromises, an automobile has to fit your needs and the needs of your family, or it will be taking a fast trip to the used-car lot.

As an extreme example, take the fellow who likes sports cars. He might be sorely tempted to buy a Mazda RX-7 — that is, if he doesn't stop to remember that he has a wife and four children who also have to get from place to place. The choice of the Mazda would be all heart and no head, and it would soon make him mis-erable. Of course, driving a big Chevy station wagon would also make him miserable, because he appreciates sporty handling characteristics. Fortunately, he can take advantage of compromises such as the Volvo wagon, which combines features that answer both his needs and his desires.

The selection process, then, starts with a realistic assessment of your driving priorities. Make a list of these priorities, and see what basic body styles and general features they lead you to. Then show your list and your conclusions to a friend who is not emotionally involved in your choice, so that you have the benefit of an objective opinion. Then and only then should you start spending time in showrooms.

Actually, it's a good idea to take even another step. Once you've got a

The Door-Slamming, Tire-Kicking Buyer

Car salespeople face the dreaded "tire kicker and door slammer." These are habits whose origins remain somewhat of a mystery.

Some of the following origins have been suggested for the practice of kicking:

- You kicked to hear the sound — solid or tinny.
- You kicked to check the front end for looseness.
- The car carried two spare tires and you kicked each to make sure they were inflated.

As for door slamming, the following answers have been tendered:

- A door was slammed to check body alignment and evidence of accident damage.
- A door was slammed through the mid-thirties to check for termites. Car bodies were framed in wood and covered with steel panels. If the wood in the door was dry-rotted or infested, there would be droppings on the running board after the door was slammed.

pretty good idea of the kind of car you want, rent one that fits the description and drive it around for a week. This will tell you a great deal about that type of car and should either confirm your decision or steer you the other way. Renting may seem expensive — but it's not nearly as expensive as getting stuck with the wrong car.

Enter the Dealer

Now it's time to start dealing with the dealers, and with their salespeople. There are three basic types of car salesmen. There are passive "order takers," who just push a pen across the form at your direction and really should be in a different line of work; unscrupulous sorts who will try to load you down with extras whether you need them or not; and, finally, conscientious individuals who can sincerely help you to build a car around your needs.

(We've already met the sharks in the last chapter, when we talked about accessories.) Obviously, you should try to latch onto the right type of salesman before the wrong type latches onto you. Start by walking into the showroom with a clear idea of what you want.

One of the first things to beware of is the "lowball" price. A salesman is lowballing you when he quotes a price that seems far too good to be true — a price at which he could hardly turn a profit. He does this to attract your interest. His next move is to call you and say, "Look, I made

"The lowball come-on": if a salesman quotes you a price that seems too low to be true, it probably is. He is probably indulging in "lowballing," a sneaky practice designed to attract your interest and commitment to a deal that could end up costing more than you would have paid elsewhere.

a mistake," or, "The sales manager tells me we really have to get more money for that car," or some other such line. When the smoke clears, your final price will probably end up being more than you would have paid elsewhere.

The standard wisdom is that a customer should comparison-shop for a car on the basis of price quotations. Actually, it makes more sense to compare general reputations, service, and location. Having paid the lowest price in town will be small consolation if you find yourself having to deal with shoddy or dishonest servicing, or if you have to drive far out of your way when it's time to bring the car into the shop. You'll wish you had paid the extra money and that you were dealing with a better operation closer at hand.

The time to compare dealers' prices is after you've settled on your options, picked your engine and transmission combination, and gone through the necessary mating dance of bargaining over the final tally, including, if need be, the trade-in allowance on your old car. A little legwork will tell you, once you've reached this point, whether you are being lowballed or overcharged.

Financing

Once the price has been settled, you'll have to shop around for the most attractive financing package. Picking a lender can be every bit as important as picking a dealer, since unnecessarily high interest can wipe out any savings you may have achieved in bargaining for the car. There *are* differences in interest — unless your credit is bad, in which case you'll have to take whatever rate you're lucky enough to get. Check the local banks, check credit unions (they're usually cheaper), and check with the dealer. Sometimes, dealers offer especially low interest rates as part of a seasonal promotion, or as an inducement to buy a specific model. Make sure, though, that the money you're going to save by taking the manufacturer's interest rate hasn't been padded into the selling price of the car. This happens all too frequently, so beware.

Buying a Used Car

The shopping procedure for a used car would be basically the same as we have outlined above — with one important addition. After you've found the car you think you want, *pay a mechanic* (don't have it done for free) to go over that car from one end to the other. Have him give you an itemized estimate of all the repair work he feels the car will need right away, along with his considered opinion as to whether the car will hold up over the long haul.

The main things to look for in evaluating a used car are indications of *collision* and *rust repair*. Mechanical problems can be fixed, and it may be well worth doing so if the price of the car is right. Bent or rusted frames are terminal, however. Keep an eye out for holes or filler in the sheet metal, parts that don't match, waves down the side of the body when you look at it in the light, and new parts on the front or rear. All of these things can conceal real trouble.

Where does a used-car dealer get his cars? Contrary to what you might believe, most of them do not come from simple trade-ins. Some are bought at wholesale, from new-car dealers who took them in on trade and sold them off as is rather than refurbish them, leaving this to the used-car dealer instead. Others are bought at auction, from a pool of cars that new-car dealers preferred not to repair. Auctions also include former rental and lease cars, as well as cars that were in what is called a "salvage pool." They would have been purchased out of the pool by a body shop or garage, rebuilt, and then placed in the auction for sale to a used-car dealer. Some of these cars are good buys, and some of them are dogs. On occasion, the rebuilders will even go so far as to take the back half of one car and the front half of another and weld them together. The problem with this tangled web of provenance is, how do you know which car came from where, and what steps it may have gone through on the way to the used-car lot?

Most states now have so-called "lemon laws," which require new- or used-car dealers either to repair or take back faulty automobiles within a prescribed amount of time. For instance, the state of Massachusetts has a law that gives the customer the right of refund if, within seven days after purchase, an automobile fails to pass the state's safety-inspection procedure and needs more than $300 or 10 percent of its total selling price in repairs. This is an example of how safety inspection can be used to the purchaser's advantage. If your state has a mandatory safety-inspection program, don't have the sticker put on at the place where you bought the car. Instead, take it yourself to be inspected at a different shop, and use your rights under the local lemon law if the car fails to pass. For a description of your rights, call the consumer protection office of your state's attorney general's office.

If you buy a car from a private party, you may be even deeper in the dark than you are when you purchase from a lot. You are on solid ground, though, if the owner can provide you with the original bill of sale (if he was in fact the sole owner) *and* the complete service records for the car. It's always a good idea to get these records, no matter whom you're buying from. They're one of the things that make it attractive to buy a former

rental or lease car directly from the rental company — Hertz, Avis, National, Budget — as these outfits put up for sale the best 25 percent of their retiring stock, complete with service records. The records will tell you which cars came back with serious complaints, and which ones served the rental market with little more than routine maintenance.

The remaining three-quarters of the rental and lease companies' turnover stock either go into the auctions we discussed earlier, or are sold as "executive purchase" or "fleet purchase" cars, through a franchised new-car dealer. Most of them are given a warranty comparable to what you'd receive with a new car.

Most of the rental and lease companies, when they sell cars from their own lots, will usually give you a new-car warranty. This warranty is generally not issued by the rental company itself, but by one of the insurance carriers, such as General Warranty Corporation, which provides warranty service for the lease and rental industry. These are large, stable companies that will not leave you in the lurch should you have a claim to settle during your period of coverage.

Selling Your Own Car

There are a number of important steps to take before you attempt to sell an automobile on your own. Wash and wax the car; touch up any paint scratches and clean the dirt from under the fenders. Wash the vinyl interior (or use upholstery cleaner on cloth), and put in new floor mats if the old ones are worn and dirty. These simple and inexpensive preparation routines can actually mean a difference of hundreds of dollars in the price an otherwise decent used car is able to command. Whether you're selling to a dealer or a private party, make sure you offer the complete file of service records, which you should keep from the time you buy a car. If a dealer sees that a car has been properly cared for, he may well be able to sell it right away to a customer who has asked him to keep his eyes open for a good used car. This means that he won't have to carry the car as inventory, and it means top dollar for you.

If you're going to advertise your car, start with the most widely read local newspapers and the weekly "shoppers." Don't overlook the bulletin board at the laundromat or supermarket, and — if you live in a rural area — simply park the car out in front of your house with a "For Sale" sign plainly visible from the road.

The fact is, though, that both selling and buying as a private party are difficult. For the seller, there's the problem of accepting cash vs. personal checks; for the buyer, there are legitimate concerns over the possibility of getting stuck with a lemon, and the lack of official recourse that accompanies the casual transaction. It's a time for sizing up not only the car, but the person you're dealing with. That is psychology, and it is outside the scope of this book.

Washing and Waxing

We all know the importance of keeping an automobile's finish free of dirt and grime. The finish on your car is not as hard as you might think, and it can be scratched easily. The tool you choose to wash your car with (brush, cloth, or sponge) can affect the life of the finish, since the wrong material can cause small surface scratches that will allow dirt and industrial fallout to get under the surface and attack the metal.

As for commercial car washes, it should be noted that many of these establishments are now getting rid of brushes and replacing them with soft cloths. The whirling brushes tended to scratch the paint on the leading edges of fenders, doors, and roofs.

If you are washing your car yourself, chose a soft, fluffy wash mitt or soft sponge. An old bath towel is also good, as long as you keep it clean and free of grit that could scratch the paint. If you drop your mitt, sponge, or towel, rinse it off before using it again.

Recycled Water
Keeping your car clean helps make it last longer. But there are occasions when in attempting to keep your car clean you could be doing it damage. The first instance is the commercial car wash that recycles water.

This type of system, if not properly designed or maintained, can spray salty water onto each car that passes through. It might be a wise idea to ask the operator of the car wash if the water is recycled; if it is, ask whether or not they check the concentration of salts and other harmful elements in the water regularly.

The other situation to avoid involves the storage of the car after a wash. About the worst thing you can do to your car's finish is to bring the car home wet and park it in a closed garage. This turns the garage into a humidity chamber and can cause the car to rust from the inside out, reducing its life and value.

AIR FLOW
AL DISPLAY

GAUGE
POINTER

Detroit

THE COMPUTERIZED CAR OF TOMORROW

AIR DRAG C

This Popular Mechanics' concept of the car computer system of
avoidance system that will be able to judge the proximit
trol of the car should an accident be immediately the proximi
munication with highway patrol computers whic
auto accidents and any other unusual situat

Hearst Magazines Public Relations
959 Eighth Avenue, N.Y., N.Y. 10019 (212) 262-6

Where Is the Car Industry Headed?

Ever since the oil embargo of 1973 gave us the first energy crisis, the automobile industry has been in a state of flux. What was once taken for granted, by manufacturers and consumers alike, can no longer be considered the norm. Everyone used to think naturally in terms of big cars, rear-wheel drive, high performance, enormous V-8 engines, ample interior space, and living-room comfort. Now, accustomed to gas at a dollar plus per gallon and well aware that the next serious fuel shortfall could be just around the corner, we've begun to adapt to smaller cars — although the larger models have by no means disappeared and are even making a modest comeback in more fuel-efficient versions.

To the Brink and Back Again

If the past ten years have been traumatic for drivers, in terms of changes in lifestyle affecting everything from shopping trips to vacations, they have been even harder on the U.S. automobile industry, which was driven to the edge of disaster in the late seventies and early eighties. Those were the worst recession years the car makers ever suffered, with record losses occurring between the years 1979 and 1982. Within the past year, the long-awaited turnaround began, with sales again striking the 10-million-unit-per-year range. This rebound means more jobs and more disposable income to sift through the entire economy. But it should not keep us from appreciating the apparently permanent changes that have come about in the way cars are manufactured, marketed, and received by the driving public.

For one thing, imports are here to stay. They currently account for roughly 30 percent of total U.S. new car sales, up from the 10- to 15-percent levels of the late sixties and early seventies. Perhaps the main reason they were able to gain such a strong hold on the market in such a short time is that foreign car manufacturers have long had to deal with circumstances that have just recently become facts of life for Detroit. The price of gasoline in Europe and Japan has been up over two and three dollars for years. People in those markets have been buying fuel-efficient cars right along. Also, most European and Japanese auto plants were completely rebuilt after World War II, and the new facilities were designed specifically for the downsized product. Meanwhile, Americans continued to build cars on assembly lines constructed in the teens, twenties, and thirties. It became increasingly difficult to maintain high standards in these antiquated shops, and the result was a drastic dropoff in the *perceived quality* of the Detroit offerings. The Japanese and European products simply began to look as if they were made better. "Perceived quality" is the term used to describe the public's impression of an automobile based on those things that are immediately apparent even to the untrained eye: door fit, alignment of chrome trim, window tightness, and the absence of rattles and leaks.

With its back against the wall, Detroit finally began to spend money to build new plants and assembly lines to turn out the smaller, fuel-efficient cars that Americans had begun to buy. And along with changes in the type of car being built, there came changes in the way the job was done. Where once parts had been bolted together, welding became the norm. Door hinges, for example, could now be permanently secured, with no chance of future alignment and adjustment problems. (Of course, when there is trouble — collision damage, say — welded joints can be trickier and more expensive to deal with than bolted-on parts.) A good deal of the new construction is now being accomplished through the use of robotics, thus assuring a uniform level of fit and finish not previously possible.

The Dealers Come Around

The revolution in the auto industry has also extended to the dealerships, which are after all the prime point of contact between the industry and the public. Back in the sixties and seventies, the dealers existed mainly as a point of sale; the salesmen themselves were all too often merely "order takers," little given to assisting buyers with the fine points of their trans-

actions. The dealers' "back shops," or service facilities, were in those days looked upon as liabilities, which many franchisees would gladly have gotten rid of if they could. Investment in the upgrading of either equipment or employee training was minimal.

Today, the smart dealers, the ones interested in survival, have cleaned up their act. They know now that both money and reputation can be made in a good service department — that, in fact, service can cover the business's overhead, while profits come out of the showroom. Parts departments have also been upgraded. All in all, there's a refreshing new attitude that the customer comes first.

A Rose Is a Rose Is a Rose . . .

There has always been keen rivalry between owners of GM cars, Ford-built cars, and other makes. Some of this rivalry seems silly in light of the real foundations of the auto industry: in fact, the companies have been so intertwined at their roots that it is difficult to unscramble them.

If anyone were to tell you that Henry Ford was the original founder of General Motors, for example, you might doubt their sanity, right? Well, read on. In 1902, Henry Ford's fledgling company was in financial straits, so he sought the advice and guidance of another Henry, Henry Leland, to help straighten things out. Leland did his job well and the Henry Ford Motor Company, as it was then called, became Leland's Cadillac Motor Car Company, the

basis of the soon-to-be-formed General Motors Corporation. In 1903 Henry Ford started again, forming the (second) Ford Motor Company, which survives to this day. Henry Leland, after leaving Cadillac in 1917, later formed the Lincoln Motor Company, where he continued to build large luxury cars . . . until he sold out later to — you guessed it — Henry Ford. The Oldsmobile, meanwhile, was the brainstorm of Ransom E. Olds. Ransom went broke, however, sold Olds, and formed the Reo Motor Company. This firm survives to this day as the maker of Reo trucks . . . and DeLorean has come and gone, and Hudson became Nash became AMC became Jeep became Renault . . .

The Return of the Big Car?

The jury is still out on the future of the automobile industry. So many things have happened so quickly — front-wheel drive, computerized engine controls, exhaust emission standards, CAFE (corporate average fuel economy) requirements, seat belts, passive restraints, impact-absorbing bumpers — that it's hard to say what will come around the corner next. Public acceptance is one of the biggest variables of all. Although the industry has spent millions on the new front-wheel-drive technology, and fwd has secured a 35- to 40-percent hold on the domestic market, we can't ignore the fact that the remainder of the buying public still prefers the larger, rear-wheel-drive cars.

It wasn't so long ago that the big car was pronounced dead: in 1981, following the dropping by GM's Pontiac Motor Division of its full-scale Bonneville and Catalina lines, Pontiac head Bill Hoglund said that "Pontiac will never again build a large car," and went on to explain that the division's emphasis would henceforth be on combining performance with fuel efficiency in smaller models. But just two years later, Hoglund had to retreat from his blunt remarks: Pontiac has introduced to the American market its large, rear-wheel-drive Canadian model, the Parisienne, which is nothing more than the pre-1981 Bonneville.

Lee Iacocca's revivified Chrysler Corporation has made a similar move, reintroducing the full-size Chrysler Newport sedan. The car is equipped with a standard 318-cubic-inch V-8, the same engine installed in the company's 1984 Plymouth Grand Fury and Dodge Diplomat models. Meanwhile, back in Stuttgart, Mercedes-Benz has announced that it will again export to the U.S. its 5-liter

V-8 gasoline engine in big sedans. The new, small, 190-series Mercedes will be sold in this country in both gas and diesel models, a switch from the respected firm's recent strategy of heavy emphasis on diesels.

The public has been reasonably enthusiastic about the big car revival, especially in view of the fact that large and small models are often priced the same. We shouldn't view this trend as an altogether backward step, though, since today's V-8s are a far cry from their gas-guzzling predecessors. Electronic ignition, computerized engine controls, and other innovations learned in the years since the fuel crises have made possible an impressive compromise between performance and economy.

The New Mechanic

Attitudes toward automobile servicing are also changing. Gone are the days when a person could buy a boxful of tools and announce that he had become a mechanic. Today's mechanic must be a sophisticated technician, conversant with the computerized controls that affect engines, transmissions, and even braking systems, as well as with the wrench-and-screwdriver jobs. There's a constant need to update skills and to keep abreast of new developments in components and repair techniques. And there is the necessary commitment to investment in high-tech equipment, such as computerized engine analyzers that can cost up to $50,000.

All of this makes it as important for the consumer to avoid the "guess and fix" mechanic as it is to steer clear of the crook who charges good money for a "wall job" — defined as an occasion in which you come back to find your car parked next to the same wall you left it at, untouched, and with a repair invoice attached. The guess-and-fix operator is a waste of time and money even if his prices are low, since he'll have you coming back time after time as he stabs in the dark at a problem he is too poorly trained to understand. Over the next few years, there will probably be a shortage of good automotive technicians, until the people who employ them begin to realize that they have to be paid in accordance with their considerable skills.

It's going to be interesting to see what happens over the next ten years. We know this much: innovations like fuel injection, turbocharging, and computers are here to stay. Also, engines will probably be in for a steady downsizing despite current trends. Aside from generally acknowledging the era of high technology and the era of limits, it's hard to say what else might be in store. But as long as you drive a car, it will make sense to know how it works, and to know what's wrong when it doesn't. That's why we opened the Last Chance Garage.

Frontrunners

Just like fascination with flight, moving over the ground at an ever-increasing rate of speed has been almost an obsession for many. The gasoline-powered motor vehicle was just in its infancy when men like Henry Ford, Louis Chevrolet, and Barney Oldfield were more interested in getting a lead on the other fellow in an auto than in empire building.

But it is evident that empire building in the auto industry goes hand in hand with this fascination for going quickly. And it seems that the power trains that we see in today's cars and the durability that they exhibit would be but a lost dream if such men had not engaged in what some might consider a frivolous rich man's pastime. For racing has provided more engineering improvements and actual testing of those ideas in the car than could have possibly been paid for by car makers aiming just at the general consumer market.

Bibliography

There are many books on the market to help the car owner and do-it-yourselfer. Out of all of them, two stand head and shoulders above the crowd. They are:

Reader's Digest Staff, ed. *Complete Car Care Manual*. New York: Random House, 1981, or directly from Reader's Digest, Pleasantville, New York 10570.

Popular Mechanics Complete Car Repair. New York: Avon Books, 1978.

For Further Reading

Boyce, Terry. *Car Interior Restoration*. Blue Ridge Summit, PA: Tab Books, 1975.

Brownell, David, ed. *Hemmings' Vintage Auto Almanac*. 5th ed. Bennington, VT: Hemmings Motor News, 1982.

―――. *Vintage Auto Almanac*. 4th ed. Bennington, VT: Hemmings Motor News, 1981.

Carley, Larry. *The Mechanics Guide to Front Wheel Drive*. Englewood Cliffs, NJ: Prentice-Hall, 1983.

Chek-Chart Editors. *See* Layne, Ken, and Roger Fennema, eds.

Chilton's Repair & Tune-up Guide (for your particular car). Radnor, PA: Chilton Book Co.

Crouse, William H. *Automotive Mechanics*. 8th ed. New York: McGraw-Hill, 1980.

Crouse, William H., and Donald L. Anglin. *The Auto Book*. 2nd ed. New York: McGraw-Hill, 1978.

―――.*Automotive Body Repair and Refinishing*. New York: McGraw-Hill, 1980.

―――. *Automotive Fuel, Lubricating and Cooling Systems*. 6th ed. New York: McGraw-Hill, 1980.

―――. Automotive Mechanics. 7th ed. New York: McGraw-Hill, 1975.

―――. *Automotive Tune-up*. New York: McGraw-Hill, 1977.

Fendell, Bob. *How to Make Your Car Last a Lifetime*. New York: Holt, Rinehart & Winston, 1981.

Halla. *Dreamboats and Milestones: Cars of the '50s*. Blue Ridge Summit, PA: Tab Books, 1981.

Kneass, Jack. *How to Buy Recreational Vehicles*. Escondido, CA: Trail-R Club of America, 1969.

―――. *How to Select a Car or Truck for Towing*. Escondido, CA: Trail-R Club of America, 1969.

Kruse Auctioneers, Inc. *The Official Price Guide to Collector Cars 1982*. 3rd ed. Collector Series. Orlando, FL: House of Collectibles, 1981.

Layne, Ken, and Roger Fennema, eds. *Master Mechanics Library*, 10 volumes. Chek-Chart Automotive Textbook Series. New York: Harper & Row.

Leigh, Bob, et al. *Automatic and Manual Transmissions, Transaxles, and Drive Trains*. Rev. ed. Roger Fennema, ed. Automobile Mechanics Refresher Course, book 5. New York: Harper & Row, 1981.

—. *Brakes, Steering, Front Suspension, Wheels, and Tires.* Roger Fennema, ed. Automobile Mechanics Refresher Course, book 4. New York: Harper & Row, 1981.

—. *Electrical Systems, Heating, and Air Conditioning.* Rev. ed. Roger Fennema, ed. Automobile Mechanics Refresher Course, book 3. New York: Harper & Row, 1981.

—. *Engines, Lubricating and Cooling Systems.* Rev. ed. Roger Fennema, ed. Automobile Mechanics Refresher Course, book 2. New York: Harper & Row, 1981.

—. *Tune-Up: Ignition and Fuel Induction Systems.* Rev. ed. Roger Fennema, ed. Automobile Mechanics Refresher Course, book 1. New York: Harper & Row, 1981.

Minor Auto Body Repair. 2nd. ed. Radnor, PA: Chilton Book Co., 1980.

Murray, Spence, ed. *Basic Auto Repair Manual.* 8th rev. ed. Basic Repair and Maintenance Series. Los Angeles: Petersen, 1977.

—. *Basic Cams, Valves and Exhaust Systems.* 4th rev. ed. Basic Repair and Maintenance Series. Los Angeles: Petersen, 1977.

—. *Basic Carburetion and Fuel Systems.* 6th rev. ed. Basic Repair and Maintenance Series. Los Angeles: Petersen, 1977.

—. *Dodge Pickup Repair.* Pickups and Vans Series. Los Angeles: Petersen, 1979.

—. *How to Tune Your Car.* 6th rev. ed. Basic Repair and Maintenance Series. Los Angeles: Petersen, 1979.

Olney, Ross R. *Listen to Your Car: An Easy Guide to Identifying Car Troubles.* New York: Walker & Co., 1981.

Rand McNally Road Atlas: United States, Canada, Mexico. Chicago: Rand McNally & Co., 1982.

Reader's Digest Staff, ed. *Drive America.* New York: Random House, 1981.

Robert Bentley, Inc. *Audi Fox Service Manual, 1973, 1974, 1975, 1976, 1977, 1978, 1979.* Cambridge, MA: Robert Bentley, Inc., 1979.

—. *Toyota Corolla 1600 Service Manual, 1975, 1976, 1977, 1978, 1979.* Cambridge, MA: Robert Bentley, Inc., 1979.

—. *Volkswagen Rabbit Jetta Diesel Service Manual 1977–1982, Including Pickup Truck.* Rev. ed. Cambridge, MA: Robert Bentley, Inc., 1982.

—. *Volkswagen Rabbit Scirocco Jetta Service Manual 1980–1982, Gasoline Models, Including Pickup Truck.* Rev. ed. Cambridge, MA: Robert Bentley, Inc., 1982.

Sclar, Deanna. *Auto Repair for Dummies.* New York: McGraw-Hill, 1976.

Weissler, Arlene, and Paul Weissler. *A Woman's Guide to Fixing the Car.* New York: Walker & Co., 1973.

Weissler, Paul. *Basic Car Repairs and Maintenance.* Popular Science Skill Book. New York: Harper & Row, 1978.

Weissler, Paul, ed. *Auto Repairs You Can Make.* New York: Arco Publishing, 1976.

Index

Note: page numbers in italics indicate illustrations

Last Chance Garage on public television
is made possible by grants from

Fram and Autolite Companies of the
Allied Automotive Group

and

State Farm Insurance Companies

Typeset in Mergenthaler Linotron
Franklin Gothic and Century Expanded
by Dix Typesetting Company, Inc.,
Syracuse, New York

Designed by Thomas Sumida,
WGBH Design, Boston